THE
HISTORY
OF
ISSUES

Child Abuse

Other Books in the History of Issues Series:

THE
HISTORY
OF
ISSUES

Child Abuse

Jean Leverich, Book Editor

GREENHAVEN PRESS
A part of Gale, Cengage Learning

GALE
CENGAGE Learning

Detroit • New York • San Francisco • New Haven, Conn • Waterville, Maine • London

GALE
CENGAGE Learning

Christine Nasso, *Publisher*
Elizabeth Des Chenes, *Managing Editor*

© 2008 Greenhaven Press, a part of Gale, Cengage Learning.

For more information, contact:
Greenhaven Press
27500 Drake Rd.
Farmington Hills, MI 48331-3535
Or you can visit our Internet site at gale.cengage.com

Articles in Greenhaven Press anthologies are often edited for length to meet page requirements. In addition, original titles of these works are changed to clearly present the main thesis and to explicitly indicate the author's opinion. Every effort is made to ensure that Greenhaven Press accurately reflects the original intent of the authors. Every effort has been made to trace the owners of copyrighted material.

Cover photograph © Parrot Pascal/Corbis Sygma.

LIBRARY OF CONGRESS CATALOGING-IN-PUBLICATION DATA

Child abuse / Jean Leverich, book editor.
    p. cm. -- (History of issues)
    Includes bibliographical references and index.
    ISBN-13: 978-0-7377-2861-3 (hardcover)
    1. Child abuse--United States. 2. Abused children--United States. 3. Child abuse-- United States--Prevention I. Leverich, Jean Marie.
    HV6626.52.C5425 2008
    362.76--dc22

                                                            2007038352

Printed in the United States of America
2 3 4 5 6 7 12 11 10 09 08

Contents

Chapter 4: Perspectives on the Treatment and Prevention of Child Abuse

Foreword

In the 1940s, at the height of the Holocaust, Jews struggled to create a nation of their own in Palestine, a region of the Middle East that at the time was controlled by Britain. The British had placed limits on Jewish immigration to Palestine, hampering efforts to provide refuge to Jews fleeing the Holocaust. In response to this and other British policies, an underground Jewish resistance group called Irgun began carrying out terrorist attacks against British targets in Palestine, including immigration, intelligence, and police offices. Most famously, the group bombed the King David Hotel in Jerusalem, the site of a British military headquarters. Although the British were warned well in advance of the attack, they failed to evacuate the building. As a result, ninety-one people were killed (including fifteen Jews) and forty-five were injured.

Early in the twentieth century, Ireland, which had long been under British rule, was split into two countries. The south, populated mostly by Catholics, eventually achieved independence and became the Republic of Ireland. Northern Ireland, mostly Protestant, remained under British control. Catholics in both the north and south opposed British control of the north, and the Irish Republican Army (IRA) sought unification of Ireland as an independent nation. In 1969, the IRA split into two factions. A new radical wing, the Provisional IRA, was created and soon undertook numerous terrorist bombings and killings throughout Northern Ireland, the Republic of Ireland, and even in England. One of its most notorious attacks was the 1974 bombing of a Birmingham, England, bar that killed nineteen people.

In the mid-1990s, an Islamic terrorist group called al Qaeda began carrying out terrorist attacks against American targets overseas. In communications to the media, the organization listed several complaints against the United States. It generally opposed all U.S. involvement and presence in the Middle East. It particularly objected to the presence of U.S. troops in Saudi Arabia, which is the home of several Islamic holy sites. And it strongly condemned the United States for supporting the nation of Israel, which it claimed was an oppressor of Muslims. In 1998 al Qaeda's leaders issued a fatwa (a religious legal statement) calling for Muslims to kill Americans. Al Qaeda acted on this order many times—most memorably on September 11, 2001, when it attacked the World Trade Center and the Pentagon, killing nearly three thousand people.

These three groups—Irgun, the Provisional IRA, and al Qaeda—have achieved varied results. Irgun's terror campaign contributed to Britain's decision to pull out of Palestine and to support the creation of Israel in 1948. The Provisional IRA's tactics kept pressure on the British, but they also alienated many would-be supporters of independence for Northern Ireland. Al Qaeda's attacks provoked a strong U.S. military response but did not lessen America's involvement in the Middle East nor weaken its support of Israel. Despite these different results, the means and goals of these groups were similar. Although they emerged in different parts of the world during different eras and in support of different causes, all three had one thing in common: They all used clandestine violence to undermine a government they deemed oppressive or illegitimate.

The destruction of oppressive governments is not the only goal of terrorism. For example, terror is also used to minimize dissent in totalitarian regimes and to promote extreme ideologies. However, throughout history the motivations of terrorists have been remarkably similar, proving the old adage that "the more things change, the more they remain the same." Arguments for and against terrorism thus boil down to the same set of universal arguments regardless of the age: Some argue that terrorism is justified to change (or, in the case of state terror, to maintain) the prevailing political order; others respond that terrorism is inhumane and unacceptable under any circumstances. These basic views transcend time and place.

Similar fundamental arguments apply to other controversial social issues. For instance, arguments over the death penalty have always featured competing views of justice. Scholars cite biblical texts to claim that a person who takes a life must forfeit his or her life, while others cite religious doctrine to support their view that only God can take a human life. These arguments have remained essentially the same throughout the centuries. Likewise, the debate over euthanasia has persisted throughout the history of Western civilization. Supporters argue that it is compassionate to end the suffering of the dying by hastening their impending death; opponents insist that it is society's duty to make the dying as comfortable as possible as death takes its natural course.

Greenhaven Press's The History of Issues series illustrates this constancy of arguments surrounding major social issues. Each volume in the series focuses on one issue—including terrorism, the death penalty, and euthanasia—and examines how the debates have both evolved and remained essentially the same over the years. Primary documents such as newspaper articles, speeches, and government reports illuminate historical developments and offer perspectives from throughout history. Secondary sources provide overviews and commentaries from a more contemporary perspective. An introduction begins each anthology and supplies essential context and background. An annotated table of contents, chronology, and index allow for easy reference, and a bibliography and list of organizations to contact point to additional sources of information on the book's topic. With these features, The History of Issues series permits readers to glimpse both the historical and contemporary dimensions of humanity's most pressing and controversial social issues.

Introduction

> "The history of childhood is a nightmare
> from which we have only recently begun
> to awaken."
>
> —Lloyd de Mause

While child abuse has taken place throughout history, it is only in relatively recent times that it has been given a name and recognized as a problem. In *Family Violence Across the Lifespan*, psychologist Ola Barnett and her colleagues note that many ancient societies, including the Greeks and Romans, openly practiced infanticide. Newborns that were not considered desirable were drowned or abandoned to die of exposure, particularly girls or those with birth defects. Christian, Muslim, and Jewish teachings all forbid infanticide, but it was still widely practiced for many centuries after these religions were well established in the Western world. Historian Maria Piers contends that infanticide was the most common crime in Europe until 1800.

Infanticide was not the only behavior earlier societies accepted that is now seen as abusive to children. Some Greek philosophers, such as Aristotle, argued that it was healthy, even beneficial, for adult men to form sexual relationships with the young boys they taught, a practice they called pedophilia (which literally means "love of boys"). Other societies did not always go so far, but it was common for women and children to be legally considered the property of their husbands or fathers, who could treat them as they saw fit. This might well include harsh physical punishments.

Far from being thought of as abusive, behaviors, such as drowning, abandoning, beating, and sexually exploiting children, were considered legitimate and normal every day interactions. Historians suggest many explanations for this. The lack of legal rights for women and children was certainly a factor. Children could be seen as an economic burden, especially those who were not healthy male children, since boys were traditionally required to help care for their parents. Prior to the development of modern technology and medicine, the early death of children to disease and accidents was more common, which may have made parents, and society in general, less willing to form attachments to individual children.

If what is now considered maltreatment was not always considered abuse, how then did these behaviors come to be considered abuse? When was child abuse discovered, exactly, and when did people start taking steps to protect children from abuse? In *Domestic Tyranny: The Making of Social Policy Against Family Violence from Colonial Times to the Present*, Elizabeth Pleck suggests that there were three distinct waves of reform against child abuse and family violence in America, in the seventeenth, nineteenth, and twentieth centuries. From 1640 to 1680, the Puritans of colonial Massachusetts enacted the first laws anywhere in the world against wife beating and "unnatural severitie" to children. From 1874 through 1890, societies for the prevention of cruelty to children created a "child rescue" movement. And, in 1962, five physicians described the common symptoms of "the battered child syndrome" in the pages of the *Journal of American Medicine.*

The "Liberties of Children"

According to Pleck, the Puritans of Massachusetts' legal doctrine, the *Body of Liberties*, provides the first reference to the "liberties of children." The law also forbade parents from exercising "any unnatural severitie" toward children. If unnatural severity occurred, children were granted "free libertie to complaine to Authorities for redresse." This was only the very beginning of a change in attitude, however, Pleck did not find any examples of a child's complaint of "unnatural severitie" ever reaching the courts. Furthermore, attitudes about what was unnaturally severe were very different in colonial times than they are today. A punishment was unnaturally severe only if it crippled or permanently injured the child. Beatings that did not permanently injure a child were acceptable. As Puritan minister Cotton Mather proclaimed, "Better whip't than damn'ed,"[1] And the Massachusetts *Body of Liberties* stipulated, as did the laws of several other colonies, that a child over the age of sixteen who cursed or struck a father or mother could be hanged to death.

In addition to being disciplined with beatings, colonial children worked very hard, according to Mary Cable, author of *The Little Darlings: A History of Child Rearing in America*. Toddlers fed chickens, wound spools of thread, and gathered kindling for the fire. By the time a girl was six years old, she could sew, knit, weave, and spin, and by the same age, a boy knew the basic principles of farming and was ready to be apprenticed to learn whatever craft or trade he would pursue for the rest of his life. Although the Massachusetts Bay Colony provided children the right to complain if they were treated with unnatural severity, life for Puritan children was quite severe. In 1641 the government made it a legal offense for children to *play*, saying that

> it is desired and will be expected that all masters of families shall see that their children and servants be industriously implied [employed] so as the mornings and evenings and other seasons may not bee lost as formerly they have bene.[2]

The following year, another order from the Massachusetts Bay government required that children who watched cattle (an undemanding task) should simultaneously perform another job such as spinning, knitting, or weaving, and that "boyes and girls bee not suffered to converse together, so as may occasion any wanton, dishonest or immodest behavior."[3]

Harsh Physical Punishment
Remained Acceptable

Corporal punishment of children, at least among the uneducated classes in America, continued to be harsh well into the nineteenth century. Pleck surveyed nineteenth-century biographies, autobiographies, and diaries, and found that most American parents used an instrument of some kind—ranging from a belt to a horsewhip—to hit their children. She found that although whippings did not happen every day, neither were they rare, and whippings were not considered child abuse. Pleck writes:

> Davy Crocket ran away from home because his father continually whipped him with a hickory stick. Robert E. Lee was raised by his aunt whose principle of childrearing was 'whip and pray and pray and whip.' John D. Rockefeller's mother tied him to a tree in the back of their home on several occasions to administer sharp whippings. Abraham Lincoln's father was often drunk and beat his son unjustifiably with his fists or a horsewhip.[4]

None of these future pioneers, statesmen, or captains of industry thought of themselves as abused children, and their experiences with discipline, Pleck suggests, were fairly typical for nineteenth-century America.

Beliefs about physical punishment of children—its necessity, methods, and effectiveness—can be traced by reviewing child-rearing literature. Three out of four advice pamphlets in sixteenth-century France and England recommended corporal punishment, according to Pleck. But by the eighteenth century, most child-rearing books recommended limiting the use of corporal punishment, and by the late nineteenth century, corporal punishment was recommended only as a "last resort." Educated nineteenth-century parents who tried to "spare the rod" experimented with punishments that operated on the child's mind rather than the body.

Attitudes Begin to Shift

Scholars of the history of childhood agree that John Locke's 1693 treatise on child rearing, *Some Thoughts Concerning the Education of Children*, made an important contribution to changing ideas of child discipline. Although Locke believed that corporal punishment was sometimes necessary and effective, he argued that children should be treated as "rational creatures" and advocated a system of child rearing based on rewards and punishment, recommending that parents praise children when they do well and withhold approval when they disobey. Unlike modern authors, Locke was not troubled that whipping might cause a child physical pain; his primary concern was that whipping was not effective and yielded only superficial obedience. Unlike parental praise or withholding of approval or affection, whipping did not lead a child to *want* to be good—only to avoid the whip.

The campaign against corporal punishment in America was not, per se, about child abuse. Although causing permanent or serious injury to a child was always considered wrong, before the Civil War (1861–1865) there was no palpable interest in defining what cruelty to children was. People believed that a parent possessed a natural right to chastise a child, which the state should not interfere with, even as corporal punishment fell out of favor. Rather, the movement against corporal punishment reflected a general trend against physical cruelty to subordinates or the helpless, as social psychologist Irwin A. Hyman suggests in *Reading, Writing and the Hickory Stick: The Appalling Story of Physical and Psychological Abuse in American Schools*. As early as 1810, many Sunday schools and orphanages, following Locke's principles of self-government, eliminated corporal punishment or restricted it to the punishment of last resort. American school reformers, led by educator Horace Mann, abolished or limited corporal punishment in schools. In 1850 Congress passed a law prohibiting flogging in the navy.

Child Welfare Becomes an Issue

The first court case of child abuse was not tried until 1874. Etta Angell Wheeler, a Methodist missionary, discovered a young girl, Mary Ellen Wilson, who was trapped in a tenement, isolated from other children, and beaten and starved on a daily basis by her stepmother. After learning that there were no laws that allowed her to remove a child from an abusive home, Wheeler brought the case to Henry Bergh, the founder of the Society for the Prevention of Cruelty to Animals. Bergh, an attorney, agreed to take the case. The jury found Mary Ellen's stepmother guilty of assault and battery. Out of Wheeler's and Bergh's efforts, the first chapter of the Society for the Prevention of Cruelty to Children was founded, and the modern American child welfare movement began.

As seen from the case of Mary Ellen Wilson, the child welfare movement grew out of the animal protection movement and even directly borrowed the same legal strategies the animal anticruelty organizations used to remove children from abusive and neglectful homes. Pleck suggests that this was not so much because the public was more concerned about animals than children but rather because the idea of child rescue involved state interference with the family unit, which was considered private, with the wife and children having no separate legal rights from husband and father. The founders of the Society for the Prevention of Cruelty to Children (SPCC) organizations were careful not to interfere with a parent's right to use corporal punishment on a child, though they did press charges in clear cases of assault such as Mary Ellen's, and the vast majority the children the SPCC placed in foster homes were victims of neglect rather than of physical abuse.

The establishment of the Society for the Prevention of Cruelty to Children in 1874 came after slaves had been freed and granted constitutional rights of citizenship and suffrage and at time when women were advocating for their own right to own property and vote. The child rescue movement grew out of a spirit of reformist zeal in post–Civil War America. Often fueled by religious principles of caring for the poor and the vulnerable, American reformers campaigned to abolish slavery, capital punishment, alcohol consumption, and prostitution. They also advocated to improve the lives of the poor, women, and children. Essentially, the child welfare movement, with the founding of many city and state Societies for the Prevention of Cruelty to Children organizations, was an upper- and middle-class reaction to the many problems created by industrialization, urbanization, poverty, and crime.

The Concept of Child Welfare Expands

The concern over an uneducated, impoverished, immigrant lower class also contributed to the antichild labor movement. The children of recent immigrants tended to live in urban communities isolated from assimilated Americans; often these children lived in poverty and were put to work at a young age. With the rise of industrialization in England and America in the eighteenth and nineteenth centuries, many poor children were sent to work in coal mines, textile mills, and other factories. Children as young as five years old were sent to work, often for long hours, and were not expected to get an education. Building on the work of the child rescue movements, a group of politicians; social workers, such as Jane Addams; and other advocates for the poor, such as photojournalist Jacob Riis and teacher Lewis Hines, formed the National Child Labor Committee in 1904 to raise public awareness over the long hours children worked in factories, mines, and farms without access to education. Child labor was not outlawed in the United States on the federal level, however, until the 1938 Fair Labor Standards Act, which set both minimum ages of employees and maximum hours that children were permitted to work.

Historians have suggested that humanitarian concern for the children of the poor was influenced by fears of illiterate, unruly immigrants and an urban criminal element and a desire to impose middle-class values on the poor. Although certainly the child rescue movement of the late nineteenth century contained elements of middle- and upper-class concerns about a growing criminal underclass from which impressionable children needed to be "rescued," the child rescue also reflected the same humanitarian impulses that called for the abolition of slavery and women's right to vote—the growing recognition that all individuals, no matter their gender, age, or race, had certain rights. By the 1890s, the SPCCs had clearly articulated the concept that children had rights—to clothing, food, shelter, affection, and an "endurable life." The 1884 annual report of the Brooklyn SPCC was representative in its description of the cruelties children had rights to be free from:

(a) All treatment or conduct by which physical pain is wrongfully, needlessly, or excessively inflicted; or

(b) By which life or limb or health is wrongfully endangered or sacrificed; or

(c) Neglect to provide such reasonable food, clothing, shelter, protection, and care as the life and well-being of the child require;

(d) The exposure of children during unreasonable hours of inclement weather, as peddlers or hawkers, or otherwise;

(e) Their employment in unwholesome, degrading, unlawful or immoral callings;

(f) Or any employment by which the powers of children are overtaxed or their hours of labor unreasonably prolonged; and

(g) The employment of children as mendicants, or the failure to restrain them from vagrancy or begging.[5] These "children's rights" form the basis of the modern child welfare system in the twentieth century. While the SPCCs of the nineteenth century were largely volunteer organizations, the early twentieth century brought about public funding for child welfare, along with a juvenile court system, probation officers, social workers, mental health professionals, and child guidance clinics. The focus of these organizations, according to psychologist Ola Barnett, was on family preservation rather than criminalizing juvenile delinquency or child abuse and neglect.

Breaking Down the Barrier of Family Privacy

The early twentieth century also saw the popularization of the ideas of Sigmund Freud, who wrote frankly about sexuality and who maintained that premature exposure to adult sexuality could cause mental health problems later in life. The rise of psychology as a recognized field—along with it the recognition of the developmental stages of childhood—led to a growing awareness of child sexual abuse as a family problem, though the therapeutic focus remained on family preservation. As Stephen Robertson, author of *Crimes Against Children: Sexual Violence and Legal Culture in New York City, 1880–1960* argues, the legal system was better prepared to deal with sexual molestation of children when a stranger or nonfamily member was the perpetrator. For the most part, abuse within the family remained a private affair. Throughout the twentieth century, "child sex abuse scandals" almost never involved the family; rather, the public's concern revolved around abuses in day-care and religious organizations—trusted "outsiders" who abused their authority.

Ideas about child abuse and the privacy of the family unit did not change much from the early nineteenth century to the 1960s, another period of enormous social reform that saw the beginning of the civil rights and women's rights movements. In 1962 C. Henry Kempe and his colleagues at the University of Colorado Medical Center published an article in the *Jour-*

nal of the American Medical Association that used medical language to describe the symptoms of "battered child syndrome." Kempe and his colleagues focused on infants and young children who were severely physically abused by their parents and argued that physical child abuse was a public health problem that medical doctors had a professional obligation to address. Kempe recommended that medical professionals work with social workers, psychiatrists, and legal professionals to protect the child and to address the family's needs and concerns.

The consequences of the medical establishment's "discovery" of child abuse were profound in opening the doors for state intervention in what was once seen as a private family matter. Like the SPCC reformers, Kempe focused on the most egregious cases of child abuse to gain attention and support for his cause. He also argued, unlike the nineteenth-century reformers, that child abuse cut across *all* social classes and that it was a middle-class problem and not just a problem of the poor, which made his concerns more immediate to middle-class taxpayers and the U.S. Congress.

A Federal Standard

Kempe's work led directly to mandatory reporting laws, in which medical professionals who suspected child abuse were required to report their suspicions to the authorities and to the modern child welfare system. Largely due to the work of physicians such as Kempe in publicizing the harm caused by physical abuse, the federal government passed the Child Abuse Prevention and Treatment Act (CAPTA) of 1974. Amended by the Keeping Children and Families Safe Act of 2003, CAPTA defines the minimum standard of child abuse and neglect as any act or failure to act on the part of a parent or caretaker which results in death, serious physical or emotional harm, or sexual abuse or exploitation, or an act or failure to act which presents an imminent risk of serious harm. CAPTA provides federal funding to states to support prevention, assessment, investigation, prosecution, and treatment activities and also provides grants to public agencies and nonprofit organizations for demonstration programs and projects.

Starting in the 1980s, social workers, such as Isabel Wolock and Bernard Horowitz and others, have questioned the effectiveness of the medical model of child abuse, noting that neglect remains the most common form of child abuse and that child neglect is overwhelmingly a problem of the poor and working classes, who often do not have access to adequate child care, health care, education, food, and other material resources and who are more likely to live in crime-infested areas and be exposed to substance abuse and criminality. Social workers Margaret G. Smith and Rowena Fong note in *Children of Neglect: When No One Cares* that people of color and the poor are overrepresented in the child welfare system and that African American children are more likely to be removed from their families than white children. These social workers and others like them argue that in order to effectively address the problems of child abuse and neglect, the child welfare system needs to focus on prevention, strengthening families, and ensuring that everyone has access to adequate resources, such as a good education, health care, child care, safe neighborhoods, and so on. They argue that children languish in foster care much longer than intended and that foster care creates additional problems for already traumatized children.

The Modern System of Child Protection

The original efforts of the Societies for the Prevention of Cruelty to Children have ballooned into a large federal bureaucracy. According to the U.S. Department of Health and Human Services, in 2005 alone an estimated 899,000 children in the United States were found to be victims of child abuse or neglect. In 2005 child protective services (CPS) agencies investigated accusations of abuse for nearly 3.6 million children. Statistically, CPS agencies found that approximately twelve out of every one thousand children in the general U.S. population had been abused. In 2005 the vast majority of abused children (63 percent) were determined to be neglected. Approximately 17 percent of maltreated children were physically abused, 9 percent were sexually abused, 7 percent were psychologically maltreated, and 2 percent were medically neglected. Although boys and girls in the United States suffer abuse at about the same rate, children under age three are more likely to be victims of abuse than older children. According to the U.S. Department of Health and Human Services, nearly 84 percent of abused children in 2005 were abused by one or both of their parents.

The controversy surrounding the history of child abuse in America and how our government has grappled with the privacy of the family and the need to intervene to protect children is but one of the issues examined in *History of Issues: Child Abuse*. In the chapters that follow, discussions focus on the origins of the child welfare movement; changing medical and psychological perspectives on child abuse; cultural and political perspectives on child abuse, including sex abuse scandals; the long-term social, psychological, and economic costs of child abuse; and the prevention and treatment of child abuse, including the foster care system, therapeutic treatment, and child protection laws. These essays provide a comprehensive overview of one of the most disturbing issues facing American society today.

Notes

1. Elizabeth Pleck, *Domestic Tyranny: The Making of Social Policy Against Family Violence from Colonial Times to the Present*. New York: Oxford University Press, 1987, p. 45.
2. Mary Cable, *The Little Darlings: A History of Child Rearing in America*. New York: Scribner, 1975, p.7.
3. Cable, *The Little Darlings*, p. 7.
4. Pleck, *Domestic Tyranny*, p. 47
5. Pleck, *Domestic Tyranny*, p. 83.

CHAPTER 1

The Origins of the Child Welfare Movement

Chapter Preface

The decades leading up to and following the American Civil War (1861–1865) produced a great burst of reformist zeal, fueled largely by a religious fervor that drove Americans to manifest their beliefs by uplifting the poor and participating in good works. In addition to abolition—the movement to abolish slavery—nineteenth-century reformers advocated, with varying degrees of success, for women's right to vote (suffrage); to end corporal punishment in schools and other public institutions, such as orphanages and alms houses; to make alcohol illegal (the temperance movement); to save animals from cruel treatment; to save girls from prostitution; to address the poverty of newly arrived, often non-English-speaking immigrants; to provide adequate housing and education for the poor; and to legislate humane working hours and conditions for those working in factories and other industrialized settings. These reform movements provided an opportunity for American women to contribute to political and social discourse about what kind of nation post–Civil War America would and should become, and women played major roles in many of these movements.

The child rescue movement of the 1870s, out of which evolved our modern child welfare system, was no exception. The first chapter of the Society of the Prevention of Cruelty to Children was founded by Mrs. Etta Angell Wheeler, a Methodist missionary, who discovered a malnourished little girl who was kept locked up all day and badly beaten by her caregivers. Shocked to discover that she had no legal recourse to remove the child from such an abusive environment, she consulted with Henry Bergh, a lawyer who had founded the Society for the Prevention of Cruelty to Animals. Bergh took the case, and the girl's stepmother was found guilty of assault and battery. The girl was placed in a foster home, and by the late nineteenth century, communities large and small had largely volunteer Societies for the Prevention of Cruelty to Children (SPCCs). These SPCCs were closely affiliated both with animal protection agencies, whose legal structure they borrowed, and with the movement to protect and provide legal counsel to battered women (where children were battered, so too, were their mothers, in many cases).

The child welfare movement also grew out of concerns about poverty, urbanization, and industrialization, as the children of the poor were often uneducated and worked long hours in factories. In the first decade of the twentieth century, social workers such as Jane Addams, founder of Hull House (which provided housing and education to the poor), and photojournalists such as Jacob Riis and Lewis Hine, documented the atrocious living and work situations of poor children, which helped create public awareness of the exploitation of children who toiled ten to fourteen hours a day in factories or farms and did not go to school. Despite their efforts, federal legislation regulating child labor was not passed until 1938.

This chapter focuses, primarily, on the period between 1873 and 1940, and on the growing awareness of children's developmental needs and their rights to decent food, housing, and education; to be cared for emotionally; and to be protected from physical and sexual abuse. The last article in the chapter argues that a medical emphasis on physical and sexual abuse in the latter part of the twentieth century has led our government to neglect poverty and other problems that the early child welfare reformers saw as critical a century ago.

The Origins of the Child Rescue Movement

Etta Angell Wheeler

Late in 1873 Etta Angell Wheeler, a Methodist missionary, received a disturbing account of child abuse in a Hell's Kitchen tenement in New York City. In this first-person account, Wheeler describes her attempts to intervene and how, when she learned that there were no laws which allowed her to rescue a child from an abusive home, she recruited the help of Henry Bergh, the president of the Society for the Prevention of Cruelty to Animals. Out of Wheeler's and Bergh's efforts, the first chapter of the Society for the Prevention of Cruelty to Children was founded, and the modern American child welfare movement began.

Late in the year 1873 there was brought to me by a poor working woman, the story of a child whose sad case inspired the founding of the first "Society for the Prevention of Cruelty to Children." The woman was a quiet, reserved Scotch woman, truthful and careful of her words. The story was that during the two previous years, there had lived in the rear tenement, 349 West 41st St., a family of three persons, a man, a woman and a little girl, supposed to be five or six years old; that during these two years the child had been a close prisoner having been seen only once by the other tenants; that she was often cruelly whipped and very frequently left alone the entire day with the windows darkened, and she locked in an inner room; that the other occupants of the house had not known to whom to make complaint, the guardian of the house, who lived on the premises, refusing to listen.

Gaining Entry

A week before, this family had moved to the rear tenement 341, on the same street. Later in the day I went to 349 and

Etta Angell Wheeler, *The Story of Mary Ellen*, American Humane Association, 1913.

heard a like story from others; then, hoping to see the child, I went to 341. The house was separated from the one in front by a narrow paved court, each of the three floors had two apartments, a living room and a bedroom in each. The living rooms were separated by a thin partition through which, during weeks to come, the cries of the child gave evidence of her unhappy life. The family I sought was on the top floor. Wondering what reason I could give for my intrusion, I knocked at the door. It was not opened. Wishing, if possible, to learn if the child was there, I knocked at the door of the adjoining apartment. A faint voice bade me "Herein." I saw a tidy room and in the dark bedroom a young German woman apparently very ill. While sitting by her bed for a short time she told me of coming with her young husband, not long before, to this land of strangers and strange speech; of her homesickness and failing health.

I asked her of her new neighbors. She had not seen them, there was a child, she had "heard it crying, perhaps it too was sick." Promising to come again, I returned to the other apartment where, after a time, the door was slightly opened and a woman's sharp voice asked my errand. I began telling her of her sick and lonely neighbor and talked on until, unconsciously, she had opened the door, so that I could step in. This I did and, being an unbidden guest, made a very brief call. I was there only long enough to see the child and gain my own impression of her condition. While still talking with the woman, I saw a pale, thin child, barefoot, in a thin, scanty dress so tattered that I could see she wore but one garment besides.

An Unloved Child

It was December and the weather bitterly cold. She was a tiny mite, the size of five years, though, as afterward appeared, she was then nine. From a pan set upon a low stool she stood washing dishes, struggling with a frying pan about as heavy as herself. Across the table lay a brutal whip of twisted leather strands and the child's meagre arms and legs bore many marks of its use. But the saddest part of her story was written on her face in its look of suppression and misery, the face of a child unloved, of a child that had seen only the fearsome side of life. These things I saw while seeming not to see, and I left without speaking to, or of, the child. I never saw her again until the day of her rescue, three months later, but I went away determined, with the help of a kind Providence, to rescue her from her miserable life.

How was this to be done? The man worked but irregularly. The woman earned no money. Their dress and living showed very little means. The postman had told the person who brought the first report to me that he left no mail for this family except, frequently, registered letters. Thinking this might mean money for keeping the child, I feared to arouse any suspicion lest the family should disappear, so I determined that no rescue should be attempted until there was fair promise of success. I asked advice. No one could tell what to do. There seemed no place of appeal. Meanwhile, it was, from the sick woman I was to learn more and more of the cruel treatment of the little girl. She grew always worse, and her bed being now against the thin wall separating the two living rooms, she could but hear much of the abusive treatment. As often as I went to see her there was a piteous story to hear. At last she was told what had first brought me to the house, and we waited and hoped together.

A Promise of Help

Weeks went by. Easter Sunday came, bright with sunshine, warm with the breath of Spring. As I went into church, passing from the brightness without to the beauty of palms, and lilies and organ strains within, the thought of the dying woman and the poor child smote upon me. I was very early and with a few flowers from the altar steps I turned away and went to spend the morning in the tenement. The child had been locked early in the dark bedroom, the Easter sunshine shut out, the man and woman had gone, and would not return till night. The poor invalid gave the flowers a pathetic welcome and as I sat by her side she told me of Easter Sundays of her childhood in the beloved Rhineland, all homesickness for which had now passed into longing for the land where sickness is not. Yet always she had wished to stay until her little fellow sufferer was rescued. We spoke of Christ and the Resurrection, of the glorious meaning of Easter Day, and we talked of the child alone in the darkness, and prayed for her release. Poor suffering woman! She knew death stood at the door, she did not yet know he was not to enter until the child she had so pitied, was free and that, in that very Easter week.

I had more than once been tempted to apply to the "Society for the Prevention of Cruelty to Animals," but had lacked courage to do what seemed absurd. However, when on the following Tuesday, a niece said: "You are so troubled over that abused child, why not go to Mr. Bergh? She is a little animal, surely." I said at once, "I will go." Within an hour I was at the society's rooms. Mr. Bergh was in his office and listened to my recital most courteously but with a slight air of amusement that such an appeal should be made there. In the end he said: "The case interests me much, but very definite testimony is needed to warrant interference between a child and those claiming guardianship. Will you not send me a written statement that, at my leisure, I may judge the weight of the evidence and may also have time to consider if this society should interfere? I promise to consider the case carefully."

It was the first promise of help and I was glad. The next morning I sent a paper giving what I had seen and heard, which was little, and the much that had been told me by others, and what seemed to me their credibility as witnesses. Going later in the day to see the sick woman, I found in her room a young man with a large official looking book under his arm. Hearing a nurse speak my name as I entered, he said to me: "I was sent to take the census in this house. I have been in every room." I inferred at once that this was a detective for Mr. Bergh. When I left the house, the young man was waiting on the sidewalk to tell me he had seen the child and was then going to Mr. Bergh with his report of her pitiable condition.

The Rescue

The next morning, Thursday, Mr. Bergh called upon me to ask if I would go to the Court House, the child having been already sent for. He expressed pleasure that he need not ask me to go to a police court, Judge Lawrence of the Supreme Court having kindly taken the case. After we had waited a short time in the Judge's Court, two officers came in, one of whom had the little girl in his arms. She was wrapped in a carriage blanket and was without other clothing than the two ragged garments I had seen her in months before. Her body was bruised, her face disfigured, and the woman, as if to make testimony sure against herself, had the day before, struck the child with a pair of shears, cutting a gash through the left eyebrow and down the cheek, fortunately escaping the eye.

The child was sobbing bitterly when brought in but there was a touch of the ludicrous with it all. While one of the officers had held the infuriated woman, the other had taken away the terrified child. She was still shrieking as they drove away and they called a halt at the first candy shop, so that she came into court weeping and terrified but waving as a weapon of defense a huge stick of peppermint candy. Poor child! It was her one earthly possession. The investigation proceeded. The child's appearance was testimony enough, little of mine was needed, and, thus, on Thursday, April 9, 1874, her rescue was accomplished. This Mr. Bergh had effected within forty-eight hours after first hearing of the case. The next day the woman, who had so often forgotten her own suffering in pity and prayer for the child, died, happy that little Mary Ellen was free. Now, for the first time, we knew the child's name.

The Prosecution

The prosecution of the woman who had so ill-treated her, followed soon. One witness was a representative of the institution from which the woman had taken the child, then less than two years old. No inquiry as to the child's welfare had been made by the institution during the intervening seven years. Record of her admission to this institution had been lost in a fire. The testimony of fellow tenants, and the damaging witness of the woman against herself, under cross-examination, secured her conviction and she was sentenced to the penitentiary for a year. When leaving the Court House I tried to thank Mr. Bergh for the rescue of the child, and asked if there could not now be a Society for the Prevention of Cruelty to Children, which should do for abused children what was being so well done for animals? He took my hand and said very emphatically: "There shall be one." Today all the world knows how well that promise was kept. The time has come for a forward movement in the welfare of children and little Mary Ellen's hand had struck the hour.

The child was rescued, but what was to be done with her? The press had given the case wide publicity, reports had drawn fanciful pictures of her beauty and attractiveness so that from every quarter from the West to Florida, and from England, came offers of adoption. The neglected, hindered child would require painstaking and patience, and those uncertain offers were declined. Some attempts to obtain her through claims of relationship were investigated by Judge Lawrence and proved fictitious. After a short time she was put in a home, not one for young children, but for grown girls, some of them wayward, who were being trained for service.

To me this was most unsatisfactory and after waiting some months I expressed my disapproval to Judge Lawrence who was now her guardian. He consulted with Mr. Bergh and soon after put Mary Ellen at my disposal. I took her to my mother near Rochester, New York, to my mother whose heart and home were always open to the needy.

A New Life for Mary Ellen

Here began a new life. The child was an interesting study, so long shut within four walls and now in a new world. Woods, fields, "green things growing," were all strange to her, she had not known them. She had to learn, as a baby does, to walk upon the ground, she had walked only upon floors, and her eye told her nothing of uneven surfaces. She was wholly un-taught; knew nothing of right and wrong except as related to punishments; did not know of the Heavenly Father; had had no companionship with children or toys. But in this home there were other children and they taught her as children alone can teach each other. They taught her to play, to be un-afraid, to know her rights and to claim them. She shared their happy, busy life from the making of mud pies up to charming birthday parties and was fast becoming a normal child.

I had taken her to my mother in June. In the autumn fol-lowing my mother died. She had asked that, after her death, my sister, living nearby, should take Mary. This she did and under her care were passed years of home and school life, of learning all good household ways; of instruction in church and Sunday school, and in gaining the love of many and the esteem of all who knew her.

When twenty-four she was married to a worthy man and has proved a good home maker and a devoted wife and mother. To her children, two bright, dutiful daughters, it has been her joy to give a happy childhood in sharp contrast to her own. If the memory of her earliest years is sad, there is this comfort that the cry of her wrongs awoke the world to the need of organized relief for neglected and abused children.

Poor Immigrant Children Live in Tenement Squalor

Jacob A. Riis

Photographer, journalist, and reformer Jacob A. Riis experienced grueling poverty after immigrating to the United States from Denmark in 1870. In 1877 he joined the New York Tribune *and was assigned to the Police Department in the slums of the lower East Side of New York City, a position he used to publicize the poor living conditions of recent immigrants to New York. His most popular works,* How the Other Half Lives: Studies Among the Tenements of New York *and* The Children of the Poor, *exposed the grinding poverty in which many Americans lived. In the following excerpt from the chapter, "The Problem of the Children," in* How the Other Half Lives, *Riis describes the appalling living conditions and neglect suffered by poor immigrant children, as well as the efforts of the Society for the Prevention of Cruelty to Children to house, feed, and educate them. In 1906 President Theodore Roosevelt called Riis "the most useful citizen of New York" and offered him positions in his administration. However, Riis preferred to continue to use his unique blend of reportage and photojournalism to advocate for better treatment of and more opportunities for the poor and their children. Riis's legacy continues with the Jacob A. Riis Neighborhood Settlement House, founded over a hundred years ago, which offers services to poor children, families, and the elderly.*

The problem of the children becomes, in these swarms, to the last degree perplexing. Their very number makes one stand aghast. I have already given instances of the packing of

Jacob A. Riis, *How The Other Half Lives: Studies Among the Tenements of New York*, New York: Charles Scribner's Sons, 1890.

the child population in [New] East Side tenements [cheap housing]. They might be continued indefinitely until the array would be enough to startle any community. For, be it remembered, these children with the training they receive—or do not receive—with the instincts they inherit and absorb in their growing up, are to be our future rulers, if our theory of government is worth anything. More than a working majority of our voters now register from the tenements. I counted the other day the little ones, up to ten years or so, in a Bayard Street tenement that for a yard has a triangular space in the centre with sides fourteen or fifteen feet long, just room enough for a row of ill-smelling closets at the base of the triangle and a hydrant at the apex. There was about as much light in this "yard" as in the average cellar. I gave up my self-imposed task in despair when I had counted one hundred and twenty-eight in forty families. Thirteen I had missed, or not found in. Applying the average for the forty to the whole fifty-three, the house contained one hundred and seventy children. It is not the only time I have had to give up such census work. I have in mind an alley—an inlet rather to a row of rear tenements—that is either two or four feet wide according as the wall of the crazy old building that gives on it bulges out or in. I tried to count the children that swarmed there, but could not. Sometimes I have doubted that anybody knows just how many there are about. Bodies of drowned children turn up in the rivers right along in summer whom no one seems to know anything about. When last spring some workmen, while moving a pile of lumber on a North River pier, found under the last plank the body of a little lad crushed to death, no one had missed a boy, though his parents afterward turned up. The truant officer assuredly does not know, though he spends his life trying to find out, somewhat illogically, perhaps, since the department that employs him admits that thousands of poor children are crowded out of the schools year by year for want of room. . . .

The Joylessness of Poor Children

With such human instincts and cravings, forever unsatisfied, turned into a haunting curse; with appetite ground to keenest edge by a hunger that is never fed, the children of the poor grow up in joyless homes to lives of wearisome toil that claims them at an age when the play of their happier fellows has but just begun. Has a yard of turf been laid and a vine been coaxed to grow within their reach, they are banished and barred out from it as from a heaven that is not for such as they. I came upon couple of youngsters in a Mulberry Street yard a while ago that were chalking on the fence their first lesson in "writin'." And this is what they wrote: "Keeb of te Grass." They had it by heart, for there was not, I verily believe, a green sod within a quarter of a mile. Home to them is an empty name. Pleasure? A gentleman once catechized a ragged class in a down-town public school on this point, and recorded the result: Out of forty-eight boys twenty had never seen the Brooklyn Bridge that was scarcely five minutes' walk away, three only had been in Central Park, fifteen had known the joy of a ride in a horse-car. The street, with its ash-barrels and its dirt, the river that runs foul with mud, are their domain. What training they receive is picked up there. And they are apt pupils. If the mud and the dirt are easily reflected in their lives, what wonder? Scarce half-grown, such lads as these confront the world with the challenge to give them their due, too long withheld, or————. Our jails supply the answer to the alternative.

A little fellow who seemed clad in but a single rag was among the flotsam and jetsam stranded at Police Headquarters one day last summer. No one knew where he came from or where he belonged. The boy himself knew as little about it as anybody, and was the least anxious to have light shed on the subject after he had spent a night in the matron's nursery. The discovery that beds were provided for boys to sleep in there, and that he could have "a whole egg" and three slices of bread for breakfast put him on the best of terms with the world in general, and he decided that Headquarters was "a bully place." He sang "McGinty" all through, with Tenth Avenue variations, for the police, and then settled down to the serious business of giving an account of himself. The examination went on after this fashion:

"Where do you go to church, my boy?"

"We don't have no clothes to go to church." And indeed his appearance, as he was, in the door of any New York church would have caused a sensation.

"Well, where do you go to school, then?"

"I don't go to school," with a snort of contempt.

"Where do you buy your bread?"

"We don't buy no bread; we buy beer," said the boy, and it was eventually the saloon that led the police as a landmark to his "home." It was worthy of the boy. As he had said, his only bed was a heap of dirty straw on the floor, his daily diet a crust in the morning, nothing else.

The Children's Aid Society

Into the rooms of the Children's Aid Society were led two little girls whose father had "busted up the house" and put them on the street after their mother died. Another, who was turned out by her step-mother "because she had five of her own and could not afford to keep her," could not remember ever having been in church or Sunday-school, and only knew the name of Jesus through hearing people swear by it She had no idea what they meant. These were specimens of the overflow from the tenements of our home-heathen that are growing up in New York's streets to-day, while tender-hearted men and women are busying themselves with the socks and the hereafter of well-fed little Hottentots [Africans] thousands of miles away. According to Canon Taylor, of York, one hundred and nine missionaries in the four fields of Persia, Palestine, Arabia, and Egypt spent one year and sixty-thousand dollars in converting one little heathen girl. If there is nothing the matter with those missionaries, they might come to New York with a good deal better prospect of success.

By those who lay flattering unction to their souls in the knowledge that to-day New York has, at all events, no brood of the gutters of tender years that can be homeless long unheeded, let it be remembered well through what effort this judgment has been averted. In thirty-seven years the Children's Aid Society, that came into existence as an emphatic protest against the tenement corruption of the young, has sheltered quite three hundred thousand outcast, homeless, and orphaned children in its lodging-houses, and has found homes in the West for seventy thousand that had none. Doubtless, as a mere stroke of finance, the five millions and a half thus spent were a wiser investment than to have let them grow up thieves and thugs. In the last fifteen years of this tireless battle for the safety of the State the intervention of the Society for the Prevention of Cruelty to Children has been invoked for 138,891 little ones; it has thrown its protection around more than twenty-five thousand helpless children, and has convicted nearly sixteen thousand wretches of child-beating and abuse. Add to this the standing army of fifteen thousand dependent children in New York's asylums and institutions, and some idea is gained of the crop that is garnered day by day in the tenements, of the enormous force employed to check their inroads on our social life, and of the cause for apprehension that would exist did their efforts flag for ever so brief a time.

Rescuing Children from Poverty

Nothing is now better understood than the rescue of the children is the key to the problem of city poverty, as presented for our solution to-day; that character may be formed where to reform it would be a hopeless task. The concurrent testimony of all who have to undertake it at a later stage: that the young are naturally neither vicious nor hardened, simply weak and undeveloped, except by the bad influences of the street, makes this duty all the more urgent as well as hopeful. Helping hands are held out on every side. To private charity the municipality leaves the entire care of its proletariat of tender years, lulling its conscience to sleep with liberal appropriations of money to foot the bills. Indeed, it is held by those whose opinions are entitled to weight that it is far too liberal a paymaster for its own best interests and those of its wards. It deals with the evil in the seed to a limited extent in gathering in the outcast babies from the streets. To the ripe fruit the gates of its prisons, its reformatories, and its workhouses are opened wide the year round. What the showing would be at this end of the line were it not for the barriers wise charity has thrown across the broad highway to ruin—is building day by day—may be measured by such results as those quoted above in the span of a single life.

The High Cost of Child Labor

Emil G. Hirsch

Until the early twentieth century, poor children in America worked long hours in factories, mines, and farms instead of attending school. In 1904 a group of politicians, social workers, and other concerned citizens formed the National Child Labor Committee (NCLC) to raise public awareness for children's rights. Two of the most famous members of the NCLC were Jane Addams, a social worker who founded Hull House to provide housing and education for the poor, and Lewis Hine, a teacher whose haunting photographs publicized the condition of child laborers. In the following essay, written in 1905, NCLC member Rabbi Emil G. Hirsch, an advocate for social justice and an early proponent of Reform Judaism, argues that it is in the employers' enlightened self-interest not to employ children, as exploitation stunts children's development and prevents them from later participating fully in either the workforce or democracy as adults. In 1916 Congress passed the Keating-Owen Act, which banned the sale of goods produced by child labor, but later that year the Supreme Court declared the act unconstitutional because it violated states' rights to regulate trade. It was not until 1938 that the Fair Labor Standards Act mandated federal regulation of minimum ages of employees and maximum hours of work for children.

Shall, under its recognized dominancy, child labor be tolerated? Has the premature employment of children in mine and mill, in shop and on the stage, the credentials of approval by the school's own central criterion? Shall self-interest not prompt the employer of labor to close the door of foundry and factory against children?

Profit and loss, let us concede, are the final determinants of the soundness or the reverse of a commercial policy. Vul-

Emil G. Hirsch, "Child Labor from the Employer's Point of View." National Child Labor Committee, Pamphlet 4, vol. XXV, no. 3, February 12–16, 1905, pp. 1–7.

garly phrased, men are not in business for their health. Is child labor profitable?

Child Labor Is Not Profitable

But little reflection will disclose that it is not. In the equation of modern industrial and commercial success, economy in time as well as in material is a dominant factor. Work to be profitable must be intense, and the degree of intensity must never be allowed to decline. This is due to the extent in which specialization has been carried out in the organizing of effort under the principle of division of labor. The colossal appetite of our steam-driven machinery must not be left unfed for the smallest particle of time. If it is, waste ensues, and waste spells loss. The investment represented by the steam engine, the consumption of fuel, the labor required for its care and supervision, depends for its profits upon the alertness with which the working force engaged upon production responds and maintains the tempo of activity. Boys and girls with undeveloped bodily frames are physically incapacitated from keeping up with the pace of productivity set as required by even the minimum of profitableness in the organization and machinery of a modern mill or mine. Their presence interferes with the speed and intensity of application on the part of adult laborers. Though nominally the wage account would seem when superficially examined to favor the employment of child labor on the score of its greater cheapness, when all the factors are considered the result bears an altogether different aspect. It is saving at the spigot and wasting at the bung. Coal, care of machinery, rent of structure, investment represented by the plant, cost of administration, insurance, and so forth, all enter into the computed cost of labor. The difference between the wage of the child and that paid an adult does by no means cover and balance the difference in profitableness between adult and child work. Grown persons by maintaining the required degree of intensity reduce the proportionate expense in fuel, machinery, rent, administration, to a point where profit is probable. Child labor will not accomplish this. The original cost of child labor is always higher than that of adult labor. Enlightened self-interest advises the elimination of the child from factory and mine.

The Many Drawbacks of Child Labor

Mentally the child is incompetent to sustain the required tension of interest without which co-operative labor is rendered almost impossible. The child mind cannot be attentive as long as that of the adult. It easily wearies; it is under constant temptation of distraction. Play is the child's natural privilege. One cannot expel nature—as a well-known Latin adage has it. Forced out of one door, the child nature will re-enter by another. The child workers will play. To maintain discipline among them is a task of exceedingly great difficulty. Still, without discipline profitable co-operation in our highy specialized system of production or distribution is impossible. Cash boys and cash girls in our mammoth department stores are for this reason not merely a source of irritation to managers and patrons alike, they are also a source of avoidable loss. The work they do could be done much more efficiently, under greater freedom from vexatious delays and errors, by a force of adults not half as numerous and therefore doubly as economic.

Again, under child labor waste of material must be expected. Labor to be profitable must be intelligent. Intelligence will pay in the end, though the first purchase price may be higher than is that for stupidity and inexperience. The child cannot be expected to be as intelligent as the adult. It is not as careful of the tools, nor as cautious in the handling of the material. It allows much to go to waste which the adult laborer always saves and turns to good account. Wise employers have begun to realize these drawbacks inherent in child labor. The number of them that plead for the privilege of employing children on the ground of the profitableness of their labor is becoming smaller every year where wise legislation has under compulsion demonstrated, as it always will, the reverse.

Child Labor Hurts Society

The opposition to restriction by the state now pretends or believes itself to be actuated by motives of social benevolence. Child labor, though not altogether profitable to the employer, is said to be advantageous to society, inasmuch as it enables many a family to keep together and in economic independence that otherwise would drift apart or, at all events, lapse into social dependency. That this assumption is fallacious [false] is not in great doubt. Child labor in competition with the labor of the parents necessarily tends to reduce the economic value of the latter. The family is not even economically profited by forcing the young prematurely into the mills and mines. If I dared venture into the moral bearings of this part of the subject, I should insist with good reason that nothing tends toward disrupting and undermining the family so perniciously as the premature economic independence of its immature members. Were even the economic fallacy not to be considered, according to which the wage of the father and mother is not affected by the labor of the child in competition with the parents this element of danger might indeed give the defenders of unrestricted liberty for exploiting child-life some pause. At all events there is one aspect that should appeal to the far-sighted enlightened employer. The employer is, or should be, a taxpayer. The tax rate is also a factor in the financial equation of his ventures. Present abuse of children, the denial to children of the opportunity to develop physically, mentally and morally, must affect the physical status and the mental and moral condition of the adults to-morrow.

Intemperance and crime make heavy drafts on the exchequer of organized society or government. But what is in most cases the producing microbe of intemperance? Is it not disordered nerves? Crime, again, has come to be known as depending upon physical conditions of body and mind. Exhaustion of childhood engenders disorder in young manhood and womanhood, which produces intemperance and all its consequent evils, and in many cases in parents the propensity to criminal and immoral indulgences. In consequence jails and insane asylums, houses of refuge for the fallen, penitentiaries must multiply. Their maintenance falls heavily on the taxpayer. This item in the ledger emphasizes the unprofitable character of child labor. Idleness in young years is not as prolific of immoral and criminal leanings as is premature employment. I have suggested the baneful effect on the nerves of the young. Who will dispute the equally pernicious influence on their morals by the surroundings in the factory or the department store? Who will deny that premature consciousness of earning capacity must foster a spirit of insubordination to parental authority? All these are elements that have made for the spread of moral contagion, which in turn is an item of expense in the budget of our municipalities and counties, ultimately assessed on the employer. Let the young attend school, let the schools be centers of rational preparation for life, keep the youth of the land out of the mills, the mines, the shops, and you will keep them later out of the dance halls, the saloons, the brothels, the jails and the penitentiaries. Give us compulsory education in conjunction with restrictions on child labor, and child saving by means of police magistrates and reformatories will soon disappear. The adult drunkards and thieves and prostitutes will become fewer, and the tax rate decrease proportionately. Let us not forget that for the welfare of society, the promotion of greater reverence for parental authority and family affection is of prime importance. Yet the factory that lures the child away from home and school, and creates in its mind the impression of economic independence from parents by turning it into a bread-winner, cannot but exert an influence fatal to home affections and virtues, and as an unintentional, but effective, enemy of family ties open the floodgates to streams of corruption, menacing the health of the nation as well as the happiness of its fathers and mothers and sons and daughters. Patriotism which looks to the preservation of school and home always pays by reducing the expense account for police and penitentiaries.

Protecting Children from Exploitation Benefits Society

And so does *justice* always pay, and therefore ought to appeal to enlightened egotism. Bitterness of social conflict and contrast is wasteful. Whatever promises to eliminate distrust and rankling sense of injustice from the relations of man to man, of employers and employees, has a financial value. It helps to increase profits. Social war and social armed truce are expensive. Abandonment of child labor cannot but make for increase of social peace. This bitterness, at all events, is removed which now must possess the child laborer's and his parents' hearts. The sons and daughters of the more fortunate classes attend school. They may play in the hours of relaxation. The children of the masses are deprived of the opportunity to become educated, to cultivate mind and soul; they are robbed of the golden smiles of innocent play and pastime. No wonder that they doubt that justice is inherent in the order of things; no wonder that they rebel against a fate which robs their children of childhood and thereby also of their full manhood and womanhood.

For that is the bitterest of all injustices that despoiled childhood invokes robbery of adolescence and virility, and strength and beauty, the promises of later years. This is certainly not compensated for by the wage paid the child. Granted for argument's sake the employer pays the child for its present time and effort, in what way does he compensate it for the loss of its future health, happiness, vigor of body, mind and soul? He does not. He cannot. Thus he receives what he does not pay for. He is unjust. Of this injustice the laborer complains. Its toleration is one of the accusations which he lays against the prevailing social order. He feels that upon him is laid a burden which he should not carry. Laws against child labor will lift that burden. They will thus make for increase in confidence, for greater social goodwill. They will thus help to make economic labor profitable to both employer and employee.

Today's Children Are Tomorrow's Citizens

Another consideration enlightened self-interest should lay near the mind of employers. Employers need "hands." Where are they to come from if children are prematurely exploited? The children of to-day ought to be the fathers and mothers of to-morrow. But they cannot be if they are devitalized in their childhood. And that is their fate where they are immolated on the altar of greed's Moloch [a Semitic god to whom children were sacrificed]. As yet immigration has not opened the eyes of many to this serious phase of the matter. But let Europe cease sending us its surplus or its scum, its energy and its misery, the short-sightedness of a policy which abuses the root and thus forestalls the growth of branches will become apparent at once. Our barren timber-robbed mountain crests monument a similar folly, but in a domain infinitely less determinative of human happiness and individual and national prosperity than that in which men and women are at stake. Deprive the children of to-day of to-morrow's strong manhood and womanhood and the employers will be deprived of strong men and women for to-morrow, and the day after. The sons and daughters of enfeebled men and women will be so stunted intellectually and so stinted physically as to be but poor substitutes for the sturdier men and women who worked yesterday. . . .

The nation which loves children and allows its children to grow up as children should, with minds trained, souls purified, and bodies kept in vigor—children that are protected in their childhood—under their parents' authority and made to know what respect and obedience imply, that nation receives from God the Law of Life; that nation will endure.

How Child Molestation Became a Crime

Stephen Robertson

In the following, Stephen Robertson, a lecturer in history at the University of Sydney in Australia, examines New York State law to argue that the idea of "child molestation" did not exist and was therefore not recognized as a crime until the mid–twentieth century. Although acts of sexual violence had previously been recognized as criminal and had been tried in the courts, Robertson explains that before the twentieth century, neither the age of the victim nor the harm to the victim was taken into consideration—just the violence of the crime. In the twentieth century, the acceptance of psychology as a science—with its emphasis on child development—increased public awareness that inappropriate touching that did not involve violence or penetration may nevertheless create lasting harm to children. By the mid–twentieth century, child molestation—an adult abusing a child's trust by touching that child in a sexual manner—was considered a crime in its own right. Robertson notes that in the mid–twentieth century, most accusations of child molestation involved adult men molesting young girls, and he concludes that despite changes in understanding child development, stereotypes about girls being more vulnerable and innocent than boys persist.

In 1927, the New York State Legislature, for the first time in almost one hundred years, created a new felony sex crime. They did so at the urging of Societies for the Prevention of the Cruelty to Children from throughout the state, whose officers drafted the bill, in consultation with the New York County district attorney [DA], in an effort to "give further protection to little children." The new offense, carnal abuse of a child, provided a punishment of up to ten years in prison for any male who "carnally abuses the body or indulges in any indecent or immoral practices with the sexual organs of a female child ten years or younger." The state's appellate courts defined "indecent or immoral practices" as any acts that involved an object or a man's hand, rather than his genitals. Carnal abuse of the body, the other form of the crime, they interpreted as referring to an act involving a man's genitals "short of intercourse," namely, an act that did not involve penetration of a girl's sexual organs.

Defining Harm to a Child

In enacting the new law, the state legislature attributed to those acts more damage to children than had previously been recognized. That additional harm had literally not been visible to legislators before. Handling the genitals and acts that did not involve genital penetration caused little, if any, physical injury, the defining feature of earlier concepts of sexual violence. Nor did they do significant damage to a child's innocence. Innocence was defined in reference to a singular sexuality centered on sexual intercourse, a penetrative act that left physical signs or caused bodily injury. From this perspective, acts such as touching and fondling were not sexual acts, and they did not introduce sexuality into a child's nature in the way that the experience of intercourse did. The injury that justified treating carnal abuse as a felony was not physical but psychological. Evidence of such injuries came from psychiatrists and psychologists who, the Michigan *Report of the Governor's Study Commission on the Deviated Criminal Sex Offender* noted, "offer substantial evidence that the traumatizing effect of a sex offense which may be considered minor may be as great as that of a sex offense involving physical force or violence." However, the law recognized only children as suffering those effects. In the case of adults who had reached sexual maturity, "acts consisting of indecent familiarities, not amounting to sexual intercourse or an attempt to have sexual intercourse" remained a misdemeanor, assault in the third degree.

In making that distinction between children and adults, the state legislature drew on notions of psychosexual development. From this perspective, acts of carnal abuse were part of a range of sexual behaviors that expressed the forms of sexuality appropriate to different stages of development. As such, even when they caused no physical injury, those acts affected how a child's sexuality developed. Subsequent amendments to the statute further elaborated that developmental framework. A 1929 amendment defined the same acts as a lesser crime, a misdemeanor, when committed with a girl between eleven and sixteen years of age. That amendment distinguished prepubescent and pubescent children, characterizing an adolescent, an individual at a more advanced stage of sexual development, as less affected by acts of carnal abuse than a young child would be. In 1933, the statute was amended again so that both forms of the offense applied to male children as well as female children. The new amendment placed children of both sexes within a common developmental framework, putting their shared age ahead of their different gender.

Changing Notions of Sexual Development

In drawing on understandings of psychosexual development to craft a gender-blind law targeted at men who committed genital acts other than intercourse, New York was at the forefront of a nationwide wave of legislative action to expand definitions of sexual violence against children. . . .

At first glance, the New York County DA's case files appear to indicate that the new notion of sexual development had won out over the older idea of innocence not only in the law but in New York City's streets and courtrooms as well. From 1931 to 1946, cases of carnal abuse made up two out of every three prosecutions involving sex crimes against children younger than eleven years of age. In the first half of the 1950s, that proportion fell but carnal abuse cases still constituted half of the total prosecutions. Although most crimes against boys continued to be cases of sodomy, with carnal abuse cases making up only one-third of the total, cases that involved boys were no longer presented differently from crimes involving girls, and they produced increasingly similar outcomes.

A closer examination, however, dispels the impression of change. Almost half of the carnal abuse cases involved acts that earlier in the century had been treated as rape. A reinterpretation of penetration, an unintended consequence of the new law, caused those cases to be categorized as carnal abuse and led to an almost complete disappearance of rape prosecutions. When it came to deciding the outcome of prosecutions, most New Yorkers continued to treat acts of carnal abuse as less harmful than rape or sexual assaults that caused physical injury. New Yorkers were not alone in taking that position. Many Americans continued to see physical injury as the defining feature of sexual violence. . . . By the late 1950s, the blunted impact of new ideas of psychosexual development was reflected in a new label applied to sex crimes against children: "child molestation."

An Unsuspecting Child

The four children arrived at the restaurant 103rd Street and Broadway early in the evening of 14 September 1941. Nine-year-old Amy Burton took her ten-month-old sister Margaret out of the baby carriage she was pushing and followed her ten-year-old brother George and Josephine Wolf, a ten-year-old friend, inside. Using the money their father had left for them at the restaurant, they bought doughnuts and then went outside to play tag on the sidewalk. While Amy and George were still inside, a man followed Josephine outside, called her over, and asked, "Do you play between your legs?" She said no. After returning to the restaurant for a glass of milk, the children set off for home. The man, a twenty-six-year-old clerk named Martin Dickens, followed them. At 104th Street and Amsterdam Avenue, he caught up with the children. Pulling Josephine on to his lap, Dickens placed his hands under her dress and in her pants, and asked, "Do you want to go down the cellar with me?" She again said no. Dickens continued to walk with them, giving Josephine a nickel. At 107th Street and Columbus Avenue, after Josephine had parted company with the group, he suggested to Amy that they go through an opening in the fence of the Lion Brewery. When she did as he asked, Amy told the grand jury, Dickens "took out his thing and put his hand under my dress." She ran back through the fence and told her brother what had happened. The two then rushed home.

Elizabeth Abel, an adult woman sitting at her window on the second floor of the building opposite the brewery, saw Amy go through the fence with Dickens. She quickly got dressed and rushed downstairs in time to see Amy emerge from the fence and disappear around the corner. Abel then followed Dickens for half an hour, until he entered a tavern on 106th Street and Manhattan Avenue. Sending a girl to call the police, she went to get Amy, whom she knew from the neighborhood, so that the girl could identify Dickens. When the police arrived, they found Dickens, Amy, and Josephine surrounded by a crowd. The officers quickly put Dickens in a squad car, and removed him to the Twenty-fourth Precinct.

Witnessing a Crime

It only took the sight of a girl going through a gap in a fence with a man to send Elizabeth Abel running for the door. She felt compelled to act even though Dickens had not forced Amy behind the fence, and the girl had not appeared distressed. Such a reaction reflected the heightened anxiety about crimes against children that marked the midcentury sex crime panic. The children who provoked that anxiety did differ from their counterparts earlier in the century, reflecting the shift in Manhattan's population. Increasing numbers of African American and Hispanic children filled the neighborhoods earlier dominated by European immigrants. For all the discussion among whites of those children's lack of innocence, especially the sexualized character of blacks, assaults on them produced reactions from their communities that matched what occurred in immigrant communities.

But the evidence that midcentury New Yorkers, as compared with the city's inhabitants of forty years earlier, had a different awareness of what constituted sexual violence is ambiguous. Elizabeth Abel and the crowd that joined her did target a man for committing an act, the touching of a child's genitals, that would not have triggered such anxiety at the turn of the century, when intercourse was the only sexual act considered harmful to a child. However, it is not at all clear that they were aware of that fact. Elizabeth Abel had acted without knowing what Dickens had done to Amy Burton.

Most witnesses at least saw the man whom they reported do something to a child, but even in that circumstance it is not clear that they knew precisely what he was doing when they took action. As in the preceding decades, New Yorkers paid less attention to boys. Witnesses reported none of the handful of carnal abuse cases involving young boys and only a small proportion of the cases of sodomy. It was men in the company of girls, and particularly a man with his hands under a girl's clothing, that aroused suspicion. But it was also the case that carnal abuse took place in the same circumstances found in child rape. Girls playing or walking in the street were approached by strangers and taken to hallways or apartments. They were assaulted in parks and by store owners in their shops, janitors in cellars, neighbors in hallways, and family friends and relatives in their own homes. Consequently, New Yorkers' willingness to report men they observed touching a child's genitals is at best ambiguous evidence that they had adopted a new view of sexual violence centered on development. . . .

Child Molestation

By the late 1950s, a new language of sexual violence was emerging, one that captured how little understandings of acts with prepubescent children had been changed by the concept of psychosexual development. In those years, the term "child molestation" began to appear regularly in the American media. An article published in *National Parent-Teacher* in 1957, for example, opened with examples of "assaults" on both girls and boys, and then quickly moved to define the problem not simply as "sex murders and brutal assaults" but as "the whole range of sex offenses against children." The authors labeled that grouping "child molestation." By prefacing the term "molestation" with the word "child," the phrase signaled the importance now given to age in determining the character of an act, both in regard to whether it was sexual and to whether it constituted sexual violence. In addition, that coupling replaced the gendered language of sexual violence of Victorian America [early-twentieth-century America] with a gender-blind language that reflected modern sexuality's emphasis on development. Child molestation also expressed the new breadth of understandings of sexuality, recognizing more acts than those encompassed by the older language of rape and its euphemisms. However, in encompassing the "whole range" of acts, the new language displaced rather than supplemented discussions of crimes against children in terms of rape.

The term "molestation" also connoted a less harmful act than that associated with the older language of rape. In more general usage, it referred to an act that was annoying or vexatious, rather than one that caused injury. Following World War II, psychiatrists and sexologists, including Alfred Kinsey, adopted the term precisely because of those connotations, using it to convey the limited harm that they believed children suffered as a result of sexual activity with adult men. Since "child molestation" was applied to the whole range of sexual acts, and not simply to nongenital acts, this usage did more than minimize the psychological damage newly recognized as attending sexual activity for children. It also played down the harm long associated with physical injuries that children suffered as a result of sexual activity.

Child Neglect Has Been Neglected for Too Long

Isabel Wolock and Bernard Horowitz

The following article was written in the 1980s, and it was the very first to argue that our society cannot effectively address child abuse if we only consider child abuse as a medical or psychological problem. Isabel Wolock and Bernard Horowitz, who are professors of social work, argue that child neglect—which they define as the failure of a child's caretaker to provide adequate health care, nutrition, shelter, education, supervision, affection or attention, and protection—is in fact a much bigger problem than the physical abuse of children, even though it does not get as much attention. The authors conclude that while physicians and legislators have paid attention to physical child abuse, which can be treated medically, child neglect is more invisible because it is closely connected to poverty and unequal access to resources such as health care, education, and fresh, nutritious food. After providing an overview of the different ways in which professionals and legislators have viewed child maltreatment, the authors argue that child neglect deserves as much attention as physical child maltreatment and that America needs to address child neglect as a social issue arising from poverty.

Child maltreatment, which has received a great deal of public attention in the last two decades, is an apt illustration of the way in which a social problem emerges, and of how and by whom it is defined. Although there tends to be agreement at a very general level that child maltreatment takes two predominant forms—child abuse and child neglect—there is considerable ambiguity, vagueness, and lack of con-

Isabel Wolock, Ph.D., and Bernard Horowitz, Ph.D., "Child Maltreatment as a Social Problem: The Neglect of Neglect," *American Journal of Orthopsychiatry*, vol. 54, no. 4, October 1984, pp. 530–43. Copyright © 1984 by the American Orthopsychiatry Association, Inc. All rights reserved. Reprinted with permission of the publisher and author.

sensus as to precisely how these two phenomena are differentiated and which specific forms of parental behavior are subsumed under each. This confusion pervades almost all contexts in which the problem is addressed, whether it be political debate, legislation, agency intervention, research, or community perceptions. Given the lack of agreement on the meanings of child abuse and neglect, it is important to specify what we mean by these terms. Child abuse refers to those intentional acts of a parent or caretaker which result, or are likely to result, in physical injury to a child. Child neglect is the failure of the child's parent or caretaker, who has the material resources to do so, to provide minimally adequate care in the areas of health, nutrition, shelter, education, supervision, affection or attention, and protection.

Child Maltreatment as Child Abuse

Child maltreatment as a social problem has come to be defined predominantly as child abuse, with child neglect having received relatively little attention and having been dealt with generally as an appendage to the problem of abuse. This is manifested in a number of arenas. First, the focus of the media has been predominantly on abuse. . . .

Political debate is another arena in which it is apparent that child maltreatment is defined primarily as physical abuse. [It is] noted that in congressional hearings prior to the passage of the Child Abuse Prevention and Treatment Act of 1974

> . . . it was clear throughout the deliberations in the Senate Subcommittee that Senator Mondale wished to restrict the definition of the problem to instances of severe physical abuse and its correlates. There are only one or two instances throughout all of the Senate Subcommittee hearings where testimony focused on parental neglect per se. . . . There were no more than two or three pages of testimony in the Senate hearings that addressed child neglect as opposed to abuse.

Similarly, the emphasis of the hearings and debate prior to the extension of the Child Abuse Prevention and Treatment Act in 1977 was upon child abuse rather than neglect. . . .

Child Maltreatment Cuts Across Social Classes

The prevailing belief concerning child maltreatment is that it cuts across all social classes to an equivalent degree, i.e., it is as much a middle-class as a lower-class phenomenon. A number of influential scholars and researchers have explicitly emphasized that child maltreatment is not a problem related to social class, while other scholars have simply not dealt with the issue of the relationship between child maltreatment and socioeconomic status. To the extent that some studies show that child maltreatment occurs to a greater degree among the poor, this finding tends to be discounted as a function of labeling and reporting patterns which are biased against the poor. As treated in the popular press and on television, child maltreatment *is* physical abuse and is more often portrayed as happening in middle-class than in lower-class families. . . .

Child Maltreatment as a Psychological Problem

The dominant view, emerging from the practice, research, and popular literature, is that child maltreatment is a disease and that the cause of the disease is a personality disturbance of the abusing parent. Literally hundreds of studies—probably the bulk of investigations into the etiology of child maltreatment—have been concerned almost exclusively with psychological variables, i.e., with discovering distinctive personality characteristics or problems of abusing parents, or deficits in the nurturing or "mothering" provided to these parents when they were children . . .-

The Emperical Fact
is the Dominant Definition

A major contradiction exists between what is known about child maltreatment and how it is defined as a social problem. Although child abuse has been the focus of professional and public attention, child neglect is the more prevalent problem. As given in the NCCAN [National Center on Child Abuse and Neglect] 1977 *Analysis*, estimates of the ratio of reported neglect to abuse cases ranged from a low of about 3:1 to highs of 9:1 and 10:1.

Nor is neglect necessarily less severe than abuse. The most recent AMA [American Medical Association] report showed that, of the total number of children who were reported to have died as a result of maltreatment in 1981, more than half (56%) died because of neglect and specifically because of the deprivation of necessities. . . .

Another area in which the data on child maltreatment clearly conflicts with how it is defined as a societal problem concerns the distribution of child maltreatment across socioeconomic groupings. Although child maltreatment certainly occurs among all socioeconomic classes there is substantial evidence that the poor are overrepresented in the statistics. . . .

According to the National Study of the Incidence and Severity of Child Abuse and Neglect:

> In comparison to the income distribution for all U.S. children, children from low income families are overrepresented in all maltreatment categories.

The report goes on to point out that the relationship is stronger for neglect than abuse; 53% of neglected children in the study and 34% of abused children came from families with incomes of less than $7,000. The types of maltreatment more commonly found among families with higher incomes ($15,000 or more) were emotional neglect and emotional abuse.

Factors Contributing to the Discrepancy

Given the substantial evidence that neglect is more prevalent than abuse, that it is just as serious, and that both neglect and abuse are associated with poverty, how do we explain the widespread preoccupation with physical abuse, the emphasis on psychological causes, and the insistence that child maltreatment is unrelated to social class? The historical events leading to the recognition of child maltreatment offer one explanation. A major factor in the emergence, legitimization, and definition of child maltreatment as a social problem was what has been described as the discovery of the "battered child syndrome" by a group of pediatric radiologists in the early 1960s, and the subsequent reporting of the new "illness" in a prestigious medical journal. . . .

It is not surprising, given the prestige and influence of the definers and its reception and recognition within the wider medical community that concern and interest in the new medical "syndrome" caught on in both professional and lay circles. . . .

In short, . . . neglect was virtually excluded from the initial phase in which child maltreatment as a contemporary social problem was recognized, from the second phase in which the problem was legitimized, and from the third in which support for the problem was mobilized. At the two later stages, in which action programs were formulated and implemented, the definition of child maltreatment was somewhat broadened to include neglect, though it appeared to be added on as an afterthought. By the 1970s most laws pertaining to the reporting of child maltreatment included neglect as well as abuse. And in 1974, when Congress passed The Child Abuse Prevention and Treatment Act, which resulted in the National Center on Child Abuse and Neglect, the act included neglect as part of the definition of child abuse. . . .

Consequences of Inattention to Neglect

At the broadest level the inattention to neglect and to the strong relationship between neglect and poverty is an indication of the failure to confront the crucial deficit in social and environmental supports required to provide adequate child care. A more adequate child care policy is the only one likely to curtail significantly the incidence and prevalence of both neglect and abuse. It would include the provision of adequate income, health care, decent housing, safe neighborhoods, employment programs, and other resources that are requisite for a positive family environment.

At the level of the agencies and professionals who provide the services to families in which maltreatment occurs, the inattention to neglect and its economic correlates, along with an emphasis on the psychological aspects of the problem, has resulted in a skewed allocation of the tiny amount of available resources—with the greater share going to case management, psychological evaluation and treatment, and, to a lesser extent, to the provision of concrete services such as homemaking and day care, the provision of emergency funds, and advocacy for the client. A large portion of the scant resources is spent to maintain a public social service structure that is supposed to provide protection to maltreated children. However, with most of its funds spent on identifying and monitoring occurrences of child maltreatment, deciding whether children should be placed, and maintaining placements, little remains with which to help families. . . .

Current Policy Is Misguided and Inadequate

This analysis suggests that the upsurge in concern about the issue of child maltreatment over the last 15 years [1969–1984] has resulted in few benefits for the vast majority of neglected children; their basic requirements remain unmet. It now seems clear that, for the most part, those who sought to alleviate child abuse—including medical and mental health practitioners, writers and researchers, media people, and political leaders who pressed for legislation and created a federal apparatus for dealing with the problem—had little idea of the dimensions and characteristics of child neglect nor any intention of presenting a program for its alleviation. Instead, what we have are incredibly swollen caseloads of protective service situations, mostly child neglect, or combinations of child abuse and neglect, reported to public child welfare agencies. These agencies lack the authority, resources, staff, and perspective to do more than function, more or less unwillingly, as part of the cover-up for the political failure to provide relevant help to these children. For example, we have long known that offering quality systematic child health care through a program such as CHAP (Child Health Assessment Program) could make a crucial difference in reducing the suffering of hundreds of thousands of lower-income children. We also know that the cost of a universal health program of this nature would be very, very low when we take into account the lessened disability rate throughout their lives that would result from early and periodic screening, diagnosis, and treatment of childhood illnesses. Many studies of neglected children have shown high rates of illness, disability, handicap, and accidents that, in part, are not adequately remedied because of the nature of the medical care provided. All too often these children receive haphazard, crisis-oriented care at overcrowded public hospitals by physicians who are overburdened, rushed, unfamiliar with the children's medical and other background information, and unlikely to be in a continuing relationship with the families. Some European countries are puzzled by the U.S. pre-occupation with assessing the numbers of maltreated children, since their universal medical care programs make it much more likely that they will get the chance to help children who are not doing well in the course of regular health care visits.

Our continued obsession with attempting to unravel the frequently obscure and diverse motivations of that small minority of parents who deliberately set out to inflict severe physical harm on their children serves to shift the definition of the social problem away from those interventions that we know are effective and helpful, toward those that are questionable, given the present state of our knowledge, social structure, organizational abilities, and willingness to provide the funds. We know this society could provide all our children with quality health care, housing, schools, food, clothing, safety, and all other material preconditions for living a decent life. While we are far from being able to understand all the reasons that lead parents to act toward their children in different ways, we do know that an essential precondition in a great many cases of substandard child care is society's failure to provide specific, concrete forms of care and support to supplement the family's own child care. We could easily afford to provide these supplemental aids to families; the provision of these deficit supplements, in and of itself, would reduce the probability that child maltreatment would be as severe a danger to the child's well being, even in those cases where it does not change parental behavior as much as we would hope.

"Theirs" and "Ours"

It takes no great insight to understand why we carefully avoid accepting the abundant evidence that indicates that readily applicable interventions in the family's material circumstances would help neglected children most: we have divided America's children into "theirs" and "ours." We don't want to spend "our" money on "their" children—though we never openly admit it. Rather, we claim that the issue is motivational; the benefits would not reach the children because of some deficit in the family, some dysfunction not amenable to appreciable amelioration with any material form of entitlement benefits. Or we turn the argument toward those who see the likelihood of increased child neglect in conditions of poverty and material deprivation, and accuse them of saying the poor love their children less than other people do. What we fail to recognize all too often is that material deprivation frequently transforms other family difficulties such as alcoholism or mental illness into a clear and present danger to the well-being of the children. Among more affluent families in which the primary caretaker has difficulties carrying out basic responsibilities, it is not at all uncommon for the family to purchase various forms of assistance, including supplemental child care in the home, to safeguard the children and keep the family intact.

Neglect is a label that is applied to one category of children from a much larger group, most of whom are living in poverty. Societal patterns of resource allocation have deprived these children of their right to the opportunity to live productive and healthy lives. To some it may seem exceptionally unrealistic to talk about the rights of children to adequate material and social resources at a time when children's supportive services and programs are reeling as a result of a heavy fiscal and ideological onslaught that has not yet come to an end. To such individuals, a more practical approach might be to advocate a policy that would attempt to salvage as much as possible. This nation was, after all, making some small but measurable progress in child nutrition, health, and education in the 1970s. However, it is our belief that we must attend now to the full dimensions of the agenda of societal changes required to give children their rights. If we fail to act now we will be ill prepared for the new campaigns we will need to launch when the political tide begins to turn. We must be ready to develop new mechanisms for resource allocation and new models of service programs for children that would avoid the categorical and deficit-focused child intervention schemes that have not met our goals up to now. When neglect as a social problem is fully recognized in its broadest dimensions within a context of poverty by professionals, political leaders, and the public, we will have made great strides toward removing a major obstacle to the preparation of such an agenda.

CHAPTER 2

Medical and Psychological Perspectives on Child Abuse

Chapter Preface

A new element entered into the public discourse on child welfare around the beginning of the twentieth century. By this point social workers, probation officers, and family courts were working to build stronger families and to rescue children from harmful situations. Increasingly, medical doctors and psychologists became interested in the long-term biological and psychological effects of early childhood abuse.

As early as 1896, the famed psychologist Sigmund Freud theorized that childhood sexual abuse was the cause of many of his patients' psychological difficulties and anxieties as adults. This implied that sexual abuse in upper- and middle-class families was much more common than was generally believed at the time. This idea shocked Freud's contemporaries and brought him so much criticism that he renounced his own idea and changed his theories, suggesting instead that children had fantasies rather than memories about sexual relationships with adults. Although Freud's later theory about children's sexual fantasies has fallen into disrepute, his original hypothesis, that sexual abuse can harm children's psychological and emotional development, informs much contemporary thinking about the long-term neurological, biological, and psychological effects of early trauma on a growing child's body and brain.

In 1962 C. Henry Kempe and colleagues sought to clarify a medical description and appropriate treatment for what they termed "battered child syndrome." The team of pediatricians and radiologists focused on the common physical symptoms of child abuse, noting the kinds of bruises and broken bones an abused child was likely to display, as well as the kinds of excuses and denials an abusive parent was likely to give and suggestions for effective ways for the medical doctor and staff to engage the abuser while protecting the child. The work of

Kempe and his colleagues is largely responsible for the passing of the Child Abuse Protection and Prevention Act (CAPTA) of 1974, which provides federal money and coordinates state resources to address child abuse.

More recently, the field of neurobiology has allowed physicians and researchers to "map" the effects of trauma on a child's brain. Research has shown that repeated trauma early in childhood actually stunts the growth of the brain, specifically the limbic system, which regulates emotion and memory. Researchers have demonstrated that as abused children grow, they have difficulty with aggression, anxiety, and depression. Judith Herman, an expert on trauma, has shown that the brains of adults who were abused as children resemble those who have survived other kinds of trauma such as torture. James Garbarino, a psychologist who focuses on abuse and aggressive behavior, has drawn similar conclusions about boys raised in abusive homes and boys raised in war-ravaged environments.

Research has shown, not surprisingly, that continuing to live in an abusive situation affects children's abilities to form intimate, trusting relations with others. These findings from the field of neurobiology support Freud's contention a century ago that early childhood abuse can lead to adult dysfunction; however, modern researchers contend that the dysfunction goes deeper than Freud believed, down to the level of fundamental changes in how an abused person's brain functions.

This chapter explores medical research on the effects of abuse on a child's body, brain, and personality.

Child Sexual Abuse Is a Source of Adult Psychological Difficulty

Sigmund Freud

Sigmund Freud is best known as the founder of psychoanalysis, a school of thought that holds that mental illness is the result of repressed or unconscious impulses, anxieties, and inner conflicts that can be understood through free association and dream interpretation, among other techniques. In his 1896 paper "The Aetiology of Hysteria," Freud attempts to understand the source of his patients' symptoms. In the late nineteenth century, the term hysteria *referred to a psychiatric condition with symptoms such as emotional excitability, anxiety, and psychosomatic illness.*

Considering the histories of eighteen adult patients (twelve female, six male) suffering from hysterical symptoms, Freud concludes that each patient shares one common characteristic: childhood sexual abuse. This was a revolutionary idea at the time. His "seduction theory," presented in "The Aetiology of Hysteria," was angrily denounced by other doctors and the general public, who did not believe that sexual abuse in the upper and middle classes was as common as Freud suggested. In 1897, in response to criticisms, Freud abandoned his seduction theory. He argued instead that the traumatic sexual events reported by his clients were imagined and that children fantasized about sexual relations with adults as part of a normal development. In modern times scientists have come to understand that childhood sexual abuse is, regretably, more common than Freud's critics believed and can cause the symptoms Freud describes.

It seems to me really astonishing that hysterical symptoms can only arise with the co-operation of memories, especially when we reflect that, according to the unanimous accounts of the patients themselves, these memories did not come into their consciousness at the moment when the symptom first made its appearance.... Where shall we get to if we follow the chains of associated memories which the analysis has uncovered? How far do they extend? Do they come anywhere to a natural end? Do they perhaps lead to experiences which are in some way alike, either in their content of the time of life at which they occur, so that we may discern in these universally similar factors the aetiology of hysteria of which we are in search?...

Past Memories of Trauma

Eventually, then, after the chains of memories have converged, we come to the field of sexuality and to a small number of experiences which occur for the most part at the same period of life—namely, at puberty. It is in these experiences, it seems, that we are to look for the aetiology of hysteria, and through them that we are to learn to understand the origin of hysterical symptoms. But here we meet with a fresh disappointment and a very serious one. It is true that these experiences, which have been discovered with so much trouble and extracted out of all the mnemic material, and which seemed to be the ultimate traumatic experiences, have in common the two characteristics of being sexual and of occurring at puberty; but in every other respect they are very different from each other both in *kind* and in *importance*. In some cases, no doubt, we are concerned with experiences which must be regarded as severe traumas—an attempted rape, perhaps, which reveals to the immature girl at a blow all the brutality of sexual desire, or the involuntary witnessing of sexual acts between parents, which at one and the same time uncovers unsuspected ugliness and wounds childish and moral sensibilities alike, and so on. But in other cases the experiences are astonishingly trivial. In one of my women patients it turned out that her neurosis was based on the experience of a boy of her acquaintance stroking her hand tenderly and, at another time, pressing his knee against her dress as they sat side by side at table, while his expression let her see that he was doing something forbidden. For another young lady, simply hearing a riddle which suggested an obscene answer had been enough to provoke the first anxiety attack and with it to start the illness. Such findings are clearly not favourable to an understanding of the causation of hysterical symptoms. If serious and trifling events alike, and if not only experiences affecting the subject's own body but visual impressions too and information received through the ears are to be recognized as the ultimate traumas of hysteria, then we may be tempted to hazard the explanation that hysterics are peculiarly constituted creatures—probably on account of some hereditary disposition or degenerative atrophy—in whom a shrinking from sexuality, which normally plays some part at puberty, is raised to a pathological pitch and is permanently retained; that they are, as it were, people who are psychically inadequate to meeting the demands of sexuality. This view, of course, leaves hysteria in men out of account. But even without blatant objections such as that, we should scarcely be tempted to be satisfied with this solution. We are only too distinctly conscious of an intellectual sense of something half-understood, unclear and insufficient.

Symptoms Lie in Earliest Memories

Luckily for our explanation, some of these sexual experiences at puberty exhibit a further inadequacy, which is calculated to stimulate us into continuing our analytic work. For it sometimes happens that they, too, lack suitability as determinants—although this is much more rarely so than with the traumatic scenes belonging to later life. Thus, for instance, let us take the two women patients whom I have just spoken of as cases in which the experiences at puberty were actually innocent ones. As a result of those experiences the patients had become subject to peculiar painful sensations in the genitals which had established themselves as the main symptoms of the neurosis. I was unable to find indications that they had been determined either by the scenes at puberty or by later scenes; but they were certainly not normal organic sensations nor signs of sexual excitement. It seemed an obvious thing, then, to say to ourselves that we must look for the determinants of these symptoms in yet other experiences, in experiences which went still further back—and that we must, for the second time, follow the saving notion which had earlier led us from the first traumatic scenes to the chains of memories behind them. In doing so, to be sure, we arrive at the period of earliest childhood, a period before the development of sexual life; and this would seem to involve the abandonment of a sexual aetiology. But have we not a right to assume that even the age of childhood is not wanting in slight sexual excitations, that later sexual development may perhaps be decisively influenced by childhood experiences? Injuries sustained by an organ which is as yet immature, or by a function which is in process of developing, often cause more severe and lasting effects than they could do in matured years. Perhaps the abnormal reaction to sexual impressions which surprises us in hysterical subjects at the age of puberty is quite generally based on sexual experiences of this sort in childhood, in which case those experiences must be of a similar nature to one another, and must be of an important kind. If this is so, the prospect is opened up that what has hitherto had to be laid at the door of a still unexplained hereditary predisposition may be accounted for as having been acquired at an early age. And since infantile experiences with a sexual content could after all only exert a psychical effect through their *memory-traces*, would not this view be a welcome amplification of the finding of psycho-analysis which tells us that *hysterical symptoms can only arise with the co-operation of memories?*. . .

I therefore put forward the thesis that at the bottom of every case of hysteria there are *one or more occurrences of premature sexual experience*, occurrences which belong to the earliest years of childhood but which can be reproduced through the work of psycho-analysis in spite of the intervening decades. I believe that this is an important finding, the discovery of a *caput Nili* [original source] in neuropathology.

The Doctor's Role in Battered Child Syndrome

Ray E. Helfer

In 1962 C. Henry Kempe and his colleagues at the University of Colorado in Denver published on important article called "Battered-Child Syndrome" in The Journal of the American Medical Association, *in which they described for the first time the telltale signs physicians should look for to determine whether a child's injuries are the result of physical child abuse. Kempe became famous for his work in educating physicians about the signs of child abuse and about working with parents suspected of abusing their children. Kempe later founded the Kempe Children's Center at the University of Colorado for the prevention and treatment of child abuse and neglect. In this article, taken from a 1968 book edited by Kempe and Ray E. Helfer called* The Battered Child, *Helfer describes the symptoms of physical child abuse and recommends how a family physician or pediatrician might talk with the child's parents and collaborate with child protection workers to protect the child.*

The family physician or pediatrician has a clear responsibility both to the child and his family. He must see this responsibility as an involvement with the total family unit and not find himself caught up in the complex situation of alienating the parents in his attempts to help the child. He must make use of every talent, both his own and others, available to him, constantly keeping in mind his role as the *family* physician . . .

Physical, nutritional, or emotional abuse is one of the most common maladies of the young child, and yet it is one which general practitioners, pediatricians, and other specialists have been unable and unwilling to diagnose. . . .

The family physician with the assistance of his psychiatric and social service colleagues must make the diagnosis, protect the child, counsel the parents, report his findings, and follow up, both medically and socially, to assure that the proper disposition has not only been made but also carried out. Many physicians are unwilling to accept this responsibility. This attitude cannot prevail much longer for the problem is too immense and the responsibilities too clear to be ignored. Emotional ties with the family, lack of understanding of his legal (much less moral) obligations, denial of the facts, inability to obtain these facts, lack of experience, and "busy attitude" are only a few of the handicaps.

The family doctor has one of the most difficult roles to play in dealing with the abused child. His first and foremost responsibility is to the child and his family. He may have to assume several other roles including marriage counselor, medical counselor, social worker, legal consultant, reporter of the facts, testifier in court, and frequently, psychiatrist. To add to his burden, the family physician is often emotionally attached to the family and child. He may have been caring for this family for many years and would thus find it difficult to fulfill his obligations. It is of the utmost importance for the physician who finds himself emotionally involved with the family of a battered child to immediately refer the child to a physician who is not so attached, preferably one who is familiar with this type of problem. All of us who have handled battered children over the years have seen unfortunate situations where the family doctor is unable to fulfill his role and yet unwilling to ask for help. . . .

The Immediate Care of the Child

Once the injury has occurred the physician's first and immediate responsibility is to the child. When the parents bring their abused or neglected child to the physician, early diagnosis and treatment is essential. Treatment not only consists of medical and surgical care but also of provisions for the protection of the child. In almost every case the first step is to admit the child to the hospital. This is done whether or not the actual medical or surgical findings are severe enough to warrant admission. The child is both patient and victim. The main reason for admitting the child to the hospital other than for assessing the degree of injury is to protect him. It should be a straight-forward admission for the purpose of evaluation. No accusations should be made and the experienced physician must restrain his zealous, and often accusing, house staff and ward nurses, who frequently blunder in their questioning of these parents. This does nothing but antagonize the parents and makes future communication most difficult.

The admission to the hospital provides time for more relaxed conversation with parents and permits a more thorough evaluation of the child. If the child is old enough, he frequently becomes less frightened and is willing to talk to the physician, thereby assisting him in his evaluation. It is common for parents to be willing and often relieved to admit a child to the hospital, if the case has been handled properly from the beginning and the house staff or the referring physician have not antagonized them. If the parents are kept well informed of everything that goes on and what is found they are usually willing to keep the child in the hospital until some definitive plan can be made. This point will not be difficult to understand if it is realized that the majority of parents who injure their children want help. If this help is offered without resorting to threats and accusations, the parents are usually most cooperative.

Medical Aspects

The medical and physical evaluation of the child must be handled thoroughly and expeditiously. Emergency care is often required if the child is acutely ill. . . .

The most common urgent problem is the subdural hematoma [a blood clot in the brain], in which case the physician should very early in the period of the child's care request the consultation of a neurosurgeon. Early handling of the subdural hematoma improves the prognosis. The neurosurgeon not only can give surgical assistance but also can provide expert opinion if the case comes to court. It is not uncommon to see documented subdural hematomas in the absence of demonstrable fractures of the skull or evidence of external trauma. The most common omission in the evaluation of these children is serial head measurements. This may be the only change noted during the early stages of this problem.

The child who has been severely beaten may present with a very acute problem related to the gastrointestinal tract such as an acute obstruction owing to a hematoma in the intestinal wall, a perforation of the intestine resulting in peritonitis or abscess formation, or lacerations of other abdominal organs. These are, of course, acute surgical emergencies and should be handled accordingly. Many children who have been battered require immediate orthopedic consultation which will improve the long-term prognosis in cases of both complete fracture as well as severe epiphyseal or metaphyseal damage owing to recurrent trauma. Traumatic eye injuries may also occur, requiring emergency care by an ophthalmologist. . . .

Every child who has had a serious unexplained injury should have X rays of the long bones, ribs, and skull. This is the physician's most important diagnostic tool and should be utilized in all situations involving possible child abuse. If the child is seen soon after the initial trauma the evidence of the trauma may be missed on the X rays. If suspicions are high, repeat X rays of the long bones in a two- or three-week period should be performed to completely rule out trauma to this area. There are a few entities that must be considered in the differential diagnosis, most of which can be ruled out by an adequate history and physical examination. . . . A radiologist who is aware of the problems of child abuse will not only be helpful in making the diagnosis but will also be most useful in the area of case finding. It is not unusual for a good radiologist when viewing routine X rays to point out suspicious areas and request additional films to confirm these suspicions.

A consultation with the hematologist is most desirable in all instances of severe bruising. In our experience it is most unusual to see bleeding tendencies in children who are battered, although a frequent explanation on the part of the parents is that "my child bruises easily." It is important, both for medical and legal reasons, to rule out the fact that the child in question does not have a bleeding disorder. Our Pediatric Hematology Section sees all of the battered children with severe bruises who are admitted to our hospital and performs a coagulation survey. It is their feeling that to rule out all known coagulation defects no less than six tests must be performed. Unless each of these is completed, the physician is deceiving himself by depending upon the results of any one of them. These are as follows: platelet count, bleeding time, clot retraction, prothrombin time, partial thromboplastin time, and tourniquet test. None of these are beyond the routine capacity of the laboratory and can be easily performed.

When a coagulation defect is found, it presents difficulties in diagnosis because of the possibility that this defect might have been responsible for the multiple ecchymoses [bruises]. We have seen only one child who has had an abnormality in any one of these studies. She was a five-year-old child who was reported to have fallen down the cellar stairs. She was covered with ecchymotic areas, some older than others. X rays were negative. She had pneumonia, possible sepsis, and pancytopenia. . . . The nutritional status, neighbor's reports, and severe ecchymoses gave every indication that the child had been severely abused, but no court action was taken and the child was sent home. Her infant brother appeared one year later at another hospital suffering from a subdural hematoma.

Cases in which children are beaten and ecchymoses are the only physical findings usually are difficult to handle. It is important, therefore, for the physician to consider the use of photography. Colored slides are most helpful in documenting findings to various law enforcement agencies and courts, as well as assisting in teaching house staff and medical students. Colored pictures may not be admissible as evidence in some courts, thereby necessitating the obtaining of black-and-white photographs as well. We are unwilling to take photographs of a child without parental or court permission. Surprisingly, we have not found it difficult to obtain parental permission if the case has been handled properly. In difficult situations court permission can usually be obtained within a short period of time.

When the medical and surgical evaluation has been completed the physician is confronted with the difficult task of gathering all the data together and making a definitive diagnosis. He should constantly be aware of *discrepancies* between the degree of trauma and the history given to explain these injuries. In many cases the diagnosis is easy. The X-ray determinations are clear cut and the physical findings reveal, without question, that the child has been severely injured. It is the indefinite case such as an isolated subdural hematoma without a history of trauma, fracture, or bruising that poses a difficult problem. What recommendations should be made to the parents or community agencies? The physician is fully aware that the subdural hematoma by and large cannot be explained on any basis other than trauma (meningitis usually not entering the picture) and yet the parents are unable or unwilling to give him the necessary history. Children with extensive ecchymoses and no other physical findings also present a difficult diagnostic problem. Every physician who has had any experience with these children has experienced the most unfortunate circumstance of having a child return home only to come back to the hospital or another hospital much more severely injured or even dead. And yet, we must not falsely accuse parents of injuring children. . . .

The Physician's Responsibility to the Parents

Once the child has been admitted to the hospital and his medical evaluation is under way the physician must turn his attention to the parents. . . . Three points seem to be most important: first, the physician must make every effort not to render judgment or become angry; second, he must realize the parents usually want help; and third, he must always keep the parents completely informed about what is going on.

It is most difficult for any individual dealing with parents who abuse children not to demonstrate some form of hostility and anger. The importance of controlling one's emotions in this situation becomes readily apparent after a case has been mishandled by an over-zealous, emotional interviewer, be he physician, medical student, police officer, or social worker. If he is able to sit down with the parents and talk with them about the problem and the child, without demonstrating any hostility, the interview will go well and the cooperation of the parents will soon become a reality. At times, in cases of severely injured children, it is best to wait several hours before talking at length with the parents about the problem. Parents are less worried and anxious, the physician is less angered, and the problem can be approached more rationally. In practically every instance where communications break down, the case has been mishandled at the outset by a physician, student, social worker, or the police.

The Importance of Honesty

I introduce myself as a staff pediatrician who is interested in talking with parents whose children have been injured. I usually begin the interview with them by explaining in some detail what has been found regarding the injuries to the child. I then ask them if they could tell me the story as to how the injuries occurred. Once they begin to talk about the child and the possible explanations for the injuries the physician is in a much better position to move into other areas of questioning. I talk with both parents individually and together while the child is in the hospital. The interview may not be completed for several days, lasting for a few minutes each day, improving rapport as well as adding new knowledge with each session.

In regard to the second point, dealing with the parents' desire for help, it must be admitted that there are times when they do not demonstrate this desire too clearly. If the physician is convinced, however, that this fact is true, the parent will eventually demonstrate in some manner his or her rather desperate longing for some form of assistance. One mother's response to my statement that I would be afraid to have her four-year-old child return home said, "You wouldn't be nearly as frightened as I would." On the other hand another mother replied, "You can go straight to hell." She finally indicated her tremendous relief when she learned the child had been placed in a foster home as a result of a court order. The rewards of working with parents who beat their children are not readily seen, and all too frequently, it may take years of follow-through of a given case before the physician is convinced that he took the right approach—and sometimes, he never is.

I have found it most helpful to be extremely honest and frank with the parents of these children. Throughout the whole interview emphasis must be toward helping the parents and the child. In the past they have rarely had anyone interested enough in them to offer assistance. If this atmosphere persists throughout the many interviews that are necessary then the antagonism, anger, and threatening aspects of the situation are diminished. . . .

Explaining the Process

After the parents are convinced that the physician is truly interested in them and their problem and has been honest with them in reporting all findings to date, it is then necessary for the physician to explain that he, as a practicing doctor in the state must by law make a report. It is at this point that many physicians find their relationship with parents strained. On one hand he has explained to them all the findings of the child's evaluations and that he is most interested in helping them, and on the other hand he then must tell them that he must make a report to a state agency. Some parents are at this point convinced that the doctor, whom they had trusted, has betrayed them. The most effective way of handling this situation is to be straightforward and frank with the parents.

I usually explain that I am in a difficult position. I tell them that I have spent these last few days or hours talking with them about their problem and that I am interested in helping them. However, because of my legal obligations that I have as a practicing physician in this state, I must send a report to a state agency on every child that I see who has been injured by other than accidental means. If the case has been handled correctly, most parents at this point will respond by saying that they knew this report had to be made. Once this hurdle has been achieved then the physician should go one step further. It is his responsibility to explain to the parents what this report actually means, to whom it will be sent, what it will say, and what will be the probable response of the recipient. If the physician does not do this, then all the work to gain rapport with the family may be lost by a single, misguided, unanticipated visit by a police officer or welfare worker.

Child Abuse Can Hurt the Brain

William J. Cromie

Harvard researcher Martin Teicher and his colleagues have done work in neurobiology that demonstrates that child abuse actually changes the structure and function of a growing child's brain and increases the risk of adult anxiety, depression, personality disorders, and suicide. In a March 2002 article in the journal Scientific American, *Teicher and his colleagues suggest that long-term child abuse damages the limbic system in the brain. The limbic system, which includes the hippocampus and the amygdala regions of the brain, plays a pivotal role in the regulation of emotion and memory; the hippocampus is the part of the brain that helps form both verbal and emotional memories, and the amygdala contributes to the emotional content of memory, such as feelings related to fear and aggression. The following article by William J. Cromie describes Teicher's research and the effects of physical and verbal abuse to children's growing brains. Although child abuse can cause devastating, long-lasting changes to brain functioning, Teicher argues that because children's brains are still growing, early detection and prevention can help minimize the damage.*

Abuse during childhood can change the structure and function of a brain, and increase the risk of everything from anxiety to suicide.

"These changes are not limited to physical and sexual abuse; there's growing evidence that even verbal assault can alter the way a developing brain is wired," says Martin Teicher, associate professor of psychiatry at Harvard Medical School.

The ominous effects are tied to reduction in the size of sensitive areas of the brain and to abnormal brain waves that mimic epilepsy.

Abuse Stunts Growth of Brain

A thick cable of nerve cells connecting the right and left sides of the brain (corpus callosum) is smaller than normal in abused children, Teicher told a meeting of science and medical writers at Harvard Medical School earlier this month [May 2003]. He and his colleagues at McLean Hospital, a psychiatric facility affiliated with Harvard, compared brain scans from 51 patients and 97 healthy children. The researchers concluded that, in boys, neglect was associated with a significant reduction in the size of the important connector. It was also abnormally small in girls who were sexually abused.

"We believe that a smaller corpus callosum leads to less integration of the two halves of the brain, and that this can result in dramatic shifts in mood and personality," Teicher explains.

Decreased Brain Activity

Brain scans also reveal decreased activity in parts of the brain concerned with emotion and attention. Patients with a history of sexual abuse or intense verbal badgering showed less blood flow in a part of the brain known as the cerebellar vermis. The vermis aids healthy people to maintain an emotional balance, but in those with a history of childhood abuse, that stabilizing function may become impaired.

Teicher points out that the vermis is strongly influenced by the environment as opposed to genetic factors. Movement stimulates it, and researchers at the National Institutes of Health found that kids with attention deficits and hyperactivity consistently show smaller than normal sizes. Teicher and his colleagues are looking into the idea that exercise might stimulate the vermis, increasing attention span and reducing hyperactivity. They plan to test this notion by comparing rocking in a hammock with more strenuous exercises.

If exercise helps, it would have an impact on a growing trend to reduce or eliminate recess and physical education in schools. Teicher suspects that children who can burn off excess energy will be better able to sit still and pay attention.

Rewiring the Brain

The connection between abuse and brain addling apparently involves stress hormones. Harsh punishment, unwanted sexual advances, belittling, and neglect are thought to release a cascade of such chemicals, which produces an enduring effect on the signals that brain cells send and receive from each other. As a result the brain becomes molded to overrespond to stress. "We know that (lab) animals exposed to stress early in life develop a brain that is wired to experience fear, anxiety, and intense fight-or-flee reactions," says Teicher. "We think the same is true of people."

Researchers peek into human brains with the help of imaging techniques and instruments that record electrical activity generated when brain cells signal each other. The results of such tests allow a comparison between the structure and functioning of normal brains and those with a confirmed history of abuse. Experiments at McLean Hosptial, for example, show that patients with a history of abuse are twice as likely to show abnormal electrical activity as nonabused people.

When right-handed victims of abuse are tested they show anomalies in the left side of their brains. (The left side controls the right side of the body and vice versa.) Studies of left-handers have yet to be done. The researchers believe that these left-side defects contribute to development of depression and memory problems in abused people.

Anomalies in electrical activity have been known to exist in incest victims since 1979. Teicher plans to look for such abnormalities in others who have been verbally abused and in those who witness violence at home. He and his colleagues have already found evidence of anxiety, depression, and brain differences in a study of 554 college students exposed to loud yelling, screaming, and belittling remarks directed at them. The latter include remarks like "You're stupid," "You'll never amount to anything," and "Why can't you be more like your cousin?" From this study, Teicher concludes that "exposure to verbal aggression may have effects as powerful as physical or nonfamilial sexual abuse."

Other research has revealed that electrical abnormalities in the brains of abused people are similar to those seen in patients with epilepsy. Some of these abuse victims even experience fake or pseudoseizures, although physical evidence of epilepsy is lacking. "It's puzzling," Teicher admits. "Childhood abuse can produce abnormal electrical brain activity that resembles a seizure state, but does not actually produce epilepsy."

Suicide on the Brain

People who have been abused as children admit to thinking about suicide more often than those who were not abused. And researchers have found a vigorous correlation between epileptic-type brain abnormalities and thoughts of suicide. "This correlation may be stronger than that which ties suicide to depression," Teicher notes. Depression is generally believed to be the prime instability that pushes people toward taking their own lives. But a study done at the National Institutes of Health found that thoughts of committing suicide actually precede depression in abused children.

"We see terribly high levels of suicide ideation in patients that show brain abnormalities that mimic epilepsy," Teicher says. "Suicidal thoughts occur four to five times more frequently in patients with these abnormalities than in healthy people."

Effects of Stress

Childhood stress has been part of human history for a very long time, so it's hard to believe that its effects on brain development are all bad. In other words, such stress should have some survival advantage. "That's an idea that we're wrestling with," Teicher says. "Does abuse modify a brain to cope with what it predicts will be a malevolent world? Will it stimulate fight or flight responses that facilitate survival and reproductive success in hostile environments?"

Teicher and his colleagues are thinking about how these ideas might be tested in animals. Such experiments might determine if, say, lab rats who experience lots of stress at an early age do better in certain situations than those who enjoy a more placid "childhood."

At this point, however, health-care workers worry more about how to handle about a million cases of childhood abuse that they find each year. Teicher advises the earliest possible assessment, monitoring, treatment, and protection from further abuse. "The younger a child, the more plastic is his or her brain, and the greater the chance of diminishing negative changes in structure or function," he says. Researchers at McLean right at this moment are writing a proposal for a grant to study how reversible the effect of abuse might be.

The Long-Term Psychological Consequences of Abuse

Judith Lewis Herman

In the following essay, excerpted from her book, Trauma and Recovery: The Aftermath of Violence—From Domestic Abuse to Political Terror, *Judith Lewis Herman discusses the psychological consequences of long-term child abuse. She suggests that when parents abuse a child, the child continues to love them even though the child is not safe. This situation, she argues, is very damaging for the abused child as he or she grows up because the child's sense of what constitutes love, trust, and safety is damaged. Herman suggests that because abused children experience an overwhelming sense of helplessness, they develop the ability to disassociate from their feelings and their experiences. Childhood abuse makes it difficult for them to know who to trust as they grow up, and they are therefore vulnerable to abuse by other people. Judith Lewis Herman is a clinical professor of psychiatry at Harvard University and an expert in the field of trauma.*

Repeated trauma in adult life erodes the structure of the personality already formed, but repeated trauma in childhood forms and deforms the personality. The child trapped in an abusive environment is faced with formidable tasks of adaptation. She must find a way to preserve a sense of trust in people who are untrustworthy, safety in a situation that is unsafe, control in a situation that is terrifyingly unpredictable, power in a situation of helplessness. Unable to care for or protect herself, she must compensate for the failures of adult care and protection with the only means at her disposal, an immature system of psychological defenses.

The pathological environment of childhood abuse forces the development of extraordinary capacities, both creative and destructive. It fosters the development of abnormal states of consciousness in which the ordinary relations of body and mind, reality and imagination, knowledge and memory, no longer hold. These altered states of consciousness permit the elaboration of a prodigious array of symptoms, both somatic and psychological. And these symptoms simultaneously conceal and reveal their origins; they speak in disguised language of secrets too terrible for words. . . .

The Abusive Environment

Chronic childhood abuse takes place in a familial climate of pervasive terror, in which ordinary caretaking relationships have been profoundly disrupted. Survivors describe a characteristic pattern of totalitarian control, enforced by means of violence and death threats, capricious enforcement of petty rules, intermittent rewards, and destruction of all competing relationships through isolation, secrecy, and betrayal. Even more than adults, children who develop in this climate of domination develop pathological attachments to those who abuse and neglect them, attachments that they will strive to maintain even at the sacrifice of their own welfare, their own reality, or their lives. . . .

In addition to the fear of violence, survivors consistently report an overwhelming sense of helplessness. In the abusive family environment, the exercise of parental power is arbitrary, capricious, and absolute. Rules are erratic, inconsistent, or patently unfair. Survivors frequently recall that what frightened them most was the unpredictable nature of the violence. Unable to find any way to avert the abuse, they learn to adopt a position of complete surrender. Two survivors describe how they tried to cope with the violence:

> Every time I tried to figure out a system to deal with her, the rules would change. I'd get hit almost every day with a

brush or a studded belt. As she was beating—I used to be in the corner with my knees up—her face changed. It wasn't like she was hitting me any more—like she was hitting someone else. When she was calm I'd show her the big purple welts and she'd say "Where'd that come from?"

There weren't any rules; the rules just kind of dissolved after awhile. I used to dread going home. I never knew what was going to happen. The threat of a beating was terrifying because we saw what my father did to my mother. There's a saying in the army: "shit rolls downhill." He would do it to her and she would do it to us. One time she hit me with a poker. After awhile I got used to it. I would roll up in a ball. . . .

Adaptation to this climate of constant danger requires a state of constant alertness. Children in an abusive environment develop extraordinary abilities to scan for warning signs of attack. They become minutely attuned to their abusers' inner states. They learn to recognize subtle changes in facial expression, voice, and body language as signals of anger, sexual arousal, intoxication, or dissociation. This nonverbal communication becomes highly automatic and occurs for the most part outside of conscious awareness. Child victims learn to respond without being able to name or identify the danger signals that evoked their alarm. In one extreme example, the psychiatrist Richard Kluft observed three children who had learned to dissociate on cue when their mother became violent.

When abused children note signs of danger, they attempt to protect themselves either by avoiding or by placating the abuser. Runaway attempts are common, often beginning by age seven or eight. Many survivors remember literally hiding for long periods of time, and they associate their only feelings of safety with particular hiding places rather than with people. Others describe their efforts to become as inconspicuous as possible and to avoid attracting attention to themselves by freezing in place, crouching, rolling up in a ball, or keeping their face expressionless. Thus, while in a constant state of autonomic hyperarousal, they must also be quiet and immobile, avoiding any physical display of their inner agitation. The result is the peculiar, seething state of "frozen watchfulness" noted in abused children. . . .

Doublethink

In this climate of profoundly disrupted relationships the child faces a formidable developmental task. She must find a way to form primary attachments to caretakers who are either dangerous or, from her perspective, negligent. She must find a way to develop a sense of basic trust and safety with caretakers who are untrustworthy and unsafe. She must develop a sense of self in relation to others who are helpless, uncaring, or cruel. She must develop a capacity for bodily self-regulation in an environment in which her body is at the disposal of others' needs, as well as a capacity for self-soothing in an environment without solace. She must develop the capacity for initiative in an environment which demands that she bring her will into complete conformity with that of her abuser. And ultimately, she must develop a capacity for intimacy out of an environment where all intimate relationships are corrupt, and an identity out of an environment which defines her as a whore and a slave.

The abused child's existential task is equally formidable. Though she perceives herself as abandoned to a power without mercy, she must find a way to preserve hope and meaning. The alternative is utter despair, something no child can bear. To preserve her faith in her parents, she must reject the first and most obvious conclusion that something is terribly wrong with them. She will go to any lengths to construct an explanation for her fate that absolves her parents of all blame and responsibility.

All of the abused child's psychological adorations serve the fundamental purpose of preserving her primary attachment to her parents in the face of daily evidence of their malice, helplessness, or indifference. To accomplish this purpose, the child resorts to a wide array of psychological defenses. By virtue of these defenses, the abuse is either walled off from conscious awareness and memory, so that it did not really happen, or minimized, rationalized, and excused, so that whatever did happen was not really abuse. Unable to escape or alter the unbearable reality in fact, the child alters it in her mind.

The child victim prefers to believe that the abuse did not occur. In the service of this wish, she tries to keep the abuse a secret from herself. The means she has at her disposal are frank denial, voluntary suppression of thoughts, and a legion of dissociative reactions. The capacity for induced trance or dissociative states, normally high in school-age children, is developed to a fine art in children who have been severely punished or abused. . . . Two survivors describe their dissociative states:

> I would do it by unfocusing my eyes. I called it unreality. First I lost depth perception; everything looked flat, and everything felt cold. I felt like a tiny infant. Then my body would float into space like a balloon.

> I used to have seizures. I'd go numb, my mouth would move, I'd hear voices, and I'd feel like my body was burning up. I thought I was possessed by devil.

Under the most extreme conditions of early, severe, and prolonged abuse, some children, perhaps those already endowed with strong capacities for trance states, begin to form separated personality fragments with their own names, psychological functions, and sequestered memories. Dissociation thus becomes not merely a defensive adaptation but the fundamental principle of personality organization. . . .

A Double Self

Not all abused children have the ability to alter reality through dissociation. And even those who do have this ability cannot rely upon it all the time. When it is impossible to avoid the reality of the abuse, the child must construct some system of meaning that justifies it. Inevitably the child concludes that her innate badness is the cause. The child seizes upon this explanation early and clings to it tenaciously, for it enables her to preserve a sense of meaning, hope, and power. If she is bad, then her parents are good. If she is bad, then she can try to be good. If, somehow, she has brought this fate upon herself, then somehow she has the power to change it. If she has driven her parents to mistreat her, then, if only she tries hard enough, she may some day earn their forgiveness and finally win the protection and care she so desperately needs. . . .

The abused child's sense of inner badness may be directly confirmed by scapegoating. Survivors frequently describe being blamed, not only for their parents' violence or sexual misconduct, but also for numerous other family misfortunes. Family legends may include stories of the harm the child caused by being born or the disgrace for which she appears to be destined. . . .

The child entrapped in this kind of horror develops the belief that she is somehow responsible for the crimes of her abusers. Simply by virtue of her existence on earth, she believes that she has driven the most powerful people in her world to do terrible things. Surely, then, her nature must be thoroughly evil. The language of the self becomes a language of abomination. Survivors routinely describe themselves as outside the compact of ordinary human relations, as supernatural creatures or nonhuman life forms. They think of themselves as witches, vampires, whores, dogs, rats, or snakes. Some use the imagery of excrement of filth to describe the inner sense of self. In the words of an incest survivor: "I am filled with black slime. If I open my mouth it will pour out. I think of myself as the sewer silt that a snake would breed upon."

By developing a contaminated, stigmatized identity, the child victim takes the evil of the abuser into herself and thereby preserves her primary attachments to her parents. Because the inner sense of badness preserves a relationship, it is not readily given up even after the abuse has stopped; rather, it becomes a stable part of the child's personality structure. Protective workers who intervene in discovered cases of abuse routinely assure child victims that they are not at fault. Just as routinely, the children refuse to be absolved of blame. Similarly, adult survivors who have escaped from the abusive situation continue to view themselves with contempt and to take upon themselves the shame and guilt of their abusers. The profound sense of inner badness becomes the core around which the abused child's identity is formed, and it persists into adult life.

This malignant sense of inner badness is often camouflaged by the abused child's persistent attempts to be good. In the effort to placate her abusers, the child victim often becomes superb performer. She attempts to do whatever is required of her. . . . None of her achievements in the world redound to her credit, however, for she usually perceives her performing self as inauthentic and false. Rather, the appreciation of others simply confirms her conviction that no one can truly know her and that, if her secret and true self were recognized, she would be shunned and reviled.

The Emotional State of the Abused Child

These deformations in consciousness, individuation, and identity serve the purpose of preserving hope and relationship, but they leave other major adaptive tasks unsolved or even compound the difficulty of these tasks. Though the child has rationalized the abuse or banished it from her mind, she continues to register its effects in her body. . . .

The emotional state of the chronically abused child ranges from a baseline of unease, through intermediate states of anxiety and dysphoria [unhappiness] to extremes of panic, fury, and despair. Not surprisingly, a great many survivors develop chronic anxiety and depression which persist into adult life. The extensive recourse to dissociative defenses may end up aggravating the abused child's dysphoric emotional state, for the dissociative process sometimes goes too far. Instead of producing a protective feeling of detachment, it may lead to a sense of complete disconnection from others and disintegration of the self. The psychoanalyst Gerald Adler names this intolerable feeling "annihilation panic." Hill describes the state in these terms: "I am icy cold inside and my surfaces are without integument, as if I am flowing and spilling and not held together any more. Fear grips me and I lose the sensation of being present. I am gone."

This emotional state, usually evoked in response to perceived threats of abandonment, cannot be terminated by ordinary means of self-soothing. Abused children discover at some point that the feeling can be most effectively terminated by a major jolt to the body. The most dramatic method of achieving this result is through the deliberate infliction of injury. The connection between childhood abuse and self-mutilating behavior is by now well documented. Repetitive self-injury and other paroxysmal forms of attack on the body seem to develop most commonly in those victims whose abuse began early in childhood.

Survivors who self-mutilate consistently describe a profound dissociative state preceding the act. Depersonalization, derealization, and anesthesia are accompanied by a feeling of unbearable agitation and a compulsion to attack the body. The initial injuries often produce no pain at all. The mutilation continues until it produces a powerful feeling of calm and relief; physical pain is much preferable to the emotional pain that it replaces. As one survivor explains: "I do it to prove I exist.". . .

Self-injury is perhaps the most spectacular of the pathological soothing mechanisms, but it is only one among many. Abused children generally discover at some point in their development that they can produce major, though temporary, alterations in their affective state by voluntarily inducing autonomic crises or extreme autonomic arousal. Purging and vomiting, compulsive sexual behavior, compulsive risk taking or exposure to danger, and the use of psychoactive drugs become the vehicles by which abused children attempt to regulate their internal emotional states. Through these devices, abused children attempt to obliterate their chronic dysphoria and to simulate, however briefly, an internal state of well-being and comfort that cannot otherwise be achieved. These self-destructive symptoms are often well established in abused children even before adolescence, and they become much more prominent in the adolescent years.

These three major forms of adaptation—the elaboration of dissociative defenses, the development of a fragmented identity, and the pathological regulation of emotional states—permit the child to survive in an environment of chronic abuse. . . .

The Child Grown Up

Many abused children cling to the hope that growing up will bring escape and freedom. But the personality formed in an environment of coercive control is not well adapted to adult life. The survivor is left with fundamental problems in basic trust, autonomy, and initiative. She approaches the tasks of early adulthood—establishing independence and intimacy—burdened by major impairments in self-care, in cognition and memory, in identity, and in the capacity to form sable relationships. She is still a prisoner of her childhood; attempting to create a new life, she reencounters the trauma. The author Richard Rhodes, a survivor of severe childhood abuse, describes how the trauma reappears in his work: "Each of my books felt different to write. Each tells a different story. . . . Yet I see that they're all repetitions. Each focuses on one or several men of character who confront violence, resist it, and discover beyond its inhumanity a narrow margin of hope. Repetition is the mute language of the abused child. I'm not surprised to find it expressed in the structure of my work at wavelengths too long to be articulated, like the resonances of a temple drum that aren't heard so much as felt in the heart's cavity.". . .

Almost inevitably, the survivor has great difficulty protecting herself in the context of intimate relationships. Her desperate longing for nurturance and care makes it difficult to establish safe and appropriate boundaries with others. Her tendency to denigrate herself and to idealize those to whom she becomes attached further clouds her judgment. Her empathic attunement to the wishes of others and her automatic, often unconscious habits of obedience also make her vulnerable to anyone in a position of power or authority. Her dissociative defensive style makes it difficult for her to form conscious and accurate assessments of danger. And her wish to relive the dangerous situation and make it come out right may lead her into reenactments of the abuse.

For all of these reasons, the adult survivor is at great risk of repeated victimization in adult life. The data on this point are compelling, at least with respect to women. The risk of rape, sexual harassment, or battering, though high for all women, is approximately doubled for survivors of childhood sexual abuse. In Diana Russell's study of women who had been incestuously abused in childhood, two-thirds were subsequently raped. Thus the child victim, now grown, seems fated to relive her traumatic experiences not only in memory but also in daily life. A survivor reflects on the unrelenting violence in her life: "It almost becomes like a self-fulfilling prophecy—you start to expect violence, to equate violence with love at an early age. I got raped six times, while I was running away from home, or hitchhiking or drinking. It kind of all combined to make me an easy target. It was devastating. The crazy thing about it is at first I felt sure [the rapists] would kill me, because if they let me live, how would they get away with it? Finally I realized they had nothing to worry about; nothing would be ever done because I had 'asked for it.'" . . .

The Risk of Repeated Abuse

More commonly, repeated abuse is not actively sought but rather is passively experienced as a dreaded but unavoidable fate and is accepted as the inevitable price of relationship. Many survivors have such profound deficiencies in self-protection that they can barely imagine themselves in a position of agency or choice. The idea of saying no to the emotional demands of a parent, spouse, lover, or authority figure may be practically inconceivable. Thus, it is not uncommon to find adult survivors who continue to minister to the wishes and needs of those who once abused them and who continue to permit major intrusions without boundaries or limits. Adult survivors may nurse their abusers in illness, defend them in adversity, and even, in extreme cases, continue to submit to their sexual demands. An incest survivor describes how she continued to take care of her abuser even as an adult: "My father got caught later on. He raped his girlfriend's daughter, and she pressed charges against him. When she threw him out, he had nowhere to go, so I took him in to live with me. I prayed he wouldn't go to jail." . . .

Survivors of childhood abuse are far more likely to be victimized or to harm themselves than to victimize other people. It is surprising, in fact, that survivors do not more often become perpetrators of abuse. Perhaps because of their deeply inculcated self-loathing, survivors seem most disposed to direct their aggression at themselves. While suicide attempts and self-mutilation are strongly correlated with childhood abuse, the link between childhood abuse and adult antisocial behavior is relatively weak. A study of over 900 psychiatric patients found that while suicidality was strongly related to a history of childhood abuse, homicidality was not.

Although the majority of victims do not become perpetrators, clearly there is a minority who do. Trauma appears to amplify the common gender stereotypes: men with histories of childhood abuse are more likely to take out their aggressions on others, while women are more likely to be victimized by others or to injure themselves. . . .

As survivors attempt to negotiate adult relationships, the psychological defenses formed in childhood become increasingly maladaptive. Double-think and a double self are ingenious childhood adaptations to a familial climate of coercive control, but they are worse than useless in a climate of freedom and adult responsibility. They prevent the development of mutual, intimate relationships or an integrated identity.

Child Abuse Can Lead to Aggressive, Antisocial Behavior

James Garbarino

In the following essay, taken from a chapter of his book, Lost Boys: Why Our Sons Turn Violent and How We Can Save Them, *James Garbarino discusses the link between child abuse and aggressive, antisocial behavior, particularly in boys and men. Garbarino, a psychologist, argues that some boys who are abused learn that aggression is a successful way of getting what they want. While most children who are abused do not become abusive themselves, many adolescents and young men who engage in aggressive or abusive behavior were abused. In this essay, Garbarino considers why past abuse can lead to abusive behavior and examines the protective factors that help abused children heal. Garbarino, codirector of the Family Life Development Center and professor of human development at Cornell University, has studied the effect of war on Palestinian and Kuwaiti children's lives and also worked extensively with boys in a juvenile correctional facility. He is considered a leading expert on lethal violence by youth and both he and* Lost Boys *were widely cited after the Columbine High School Shooting in 1999.*

Nothing tells us more about the link between child maltreatment and aggressive bad behavior than the research of psychologist Kenneth Dodge and his colleagues at Vanderbilt University. Child maltreatment teaches children to adapt their behavior and thinking to the harsh fact that those who are in charge of caring for them are the same people who hurt, terrify, ignore, and attack them. This very adaptation ultimately becomes the source of their problems in later years.

According to the studies by Dodge and his colleagues, *children who are maltreated are much more likely than non-maltreated to develop a chronic pattern of bad behavior and aggression.* The key lies in the fact that the child comes to understand how the world works through the lens of his own abuse. Put another way, a child's worldview is a matter of how he draws his social map.

Of course, all children develop social maps and codes of behavior, which are initially the products of their experiences as filtered by their temperament. For most children, the social map portrays the world in positive terms: *I can trust people. If I behave well, I will be treated well. I am lovable. I have allies in the world.* And as a result, these children naturally develop benign codes of behavior: *Listen to adults. Cooperation pays off. Be patient. Share. I will keep my hands to myself.* Such social maps and codes of behavior give direction to life.

Negative Social Maps

Abused children develop their social maps by adapting to an abusive environment. The more they learn these lessons, the more likely it is that they will learn a code that is compatible with a pattern of bad behavior and aggression by the time they are eight years old. There are four specific elements of this code that are especially important for subsequent behavior and development.

1. *Children become hypersensitive to negative social cues.*
   Thomas sits with me watching staff and other kids pass by the window of the interview room. As each one goes by, he has something to say that marks them as dangerous. "This one looked at me funny yesterday," he says. "That one is bothering me," he tells me. "See that guy there? I think he's got a blade hidden." No one escapes his watchful eye. He continues: "Just the other day one of the teachers insulted me. She made me feel stupid for asking a question in a class."

2. *Children become oblivious to positive social cues.* Michael cannot think of one race thing that anyone has done for him in the pest year of his incarceration, yet I know of at least three staff members who have gone out of their way to offer him a kind word or some special bit of help. And I know that the teacher who Thomas says insulted him makes a point of praising him whenever she can.

3. *Children develop a repertory of aggressive behaviors that are readily accessible and can be easily invoked.* Malcolm tells me, "I know how to fight. Someone touches me, I'm going to finish it. Somebody hits me, I hit him back twice as hard. I hit him until he bleeds, 'cause that way he's not going to hit me again. You know what I mean." I do.

4. *Children draw the conclusion that aggression is a successful way of getting what they want.* Dennis says, "I learned early in life that there's winners and there's losers. The winners end up on top. The losers bleed. I can take care of myself if I need to. I know the rules." He learned that lesson first at home, at the hands of his parents, and it was later reinforced on the playground and on the street.

The code of violent boys and the social maps it reflects partially explain the nature of their bad behavior. They are not dumb. They observe and they experience, and they draw conclusions based on what they see and feel. Specific experiences become general patterns that together become the lenses through which they see the world. In early childhood they begin to draw negative psychological conclusions about the world and about their place in that world. With these negative social maps in place, they act accordingly.

According to psychologist Alan Kazdin, about 4 to 7 percent of kids exhibit chronic patterns of bad behavior and aggression that are serious enough to constitute a diagnosable mental health problem, such as Conduct Disorder. Boys are anywhere from three to four times as likely to display this pattern as are girls. How specifically are the social maps that abused kids develop linked to their later bad behavior and aggression? Dodge and colleagues found that if a child is maltreated and develops none of the four critical code elements associated with a negative social map the odds that he will exhibit chronic bad behavior and aggression are 5 percent, about what's normal for the population as a whole. But if the child manifests at least three of the four code elements, we can expect a sevenfold increase in the risk that the child will exhibit the pattern of chronic bad behavior and aggression that defines Conduct Disorder.

Why Don't Most Abused Kids Develop Bad Behavior and Aggression

While most kids don't become violent criminals, of course, it is true that the majority of boys incarcerated for violent crimes were subject to abuse or neglect as children. But what about the abused kids who don't develop the negative social maps and don't develop chronic bad behavior and aggression? What about them?

Only 35 percent of abused kids with negative and aggressive social maps become violent, according to Dodge. Why is it that 65 percent of the kids who have been abused and have negative social maps do not develop a pattern of bad behavior and aggression? Why do some boys who are abused develop some or all of the self-defeating behaviors and activities that characterize bad boys while others do not? Some children probably respond by developing other kinds of problems, perhaps confining their response to the internalizing problems of depression, low self-esteem, self-destructive behavior, and bodily troubles like headaches and stomachaches.

Some children do seem resilient. Why? With some boys, the answer seems clearly linked to a compensatory relationship—that is, a relationship with a devoted grandmother, a father who balances out an abusing mother, a loving mother who compensates for an abusive father, perhaps someone outside the family who is positively crazy about the child and who does not let the child's emotional life wither on the vine but lovingly helps redraw the child's social maps. The resilience of some children is due to the fact that the abuse they experience is limited to physical assault and they are able to feel a measure of love and acceptance from their parents at the times when they are not abused.

Some at-risk children are saved by an intervention program, perhaps a highly effective early childhood education program or the work of a child guidance clinic. Therapists can help children improve their attitudes and their behaviors. Some of the same psychologists who study the origins of bad behavior and aggression in children also remedy those problems. . . .

Beyond Social Maps: Dissociation and Emotional Numbing

There is more to the link between child maltreatment and the development of violence and antisocial behavior than its effects on the child's social map, however. Actual brain damage may be involved, perhaps accounting for some of the unexplained differences between children who become violent youth and those who don't. Baylor University psychiatrist Bruce Perry and his colleagues documented damaging effects to children's brains as a result of the trauma of child abuse. Particularly vulnerable to such damage is the cortex of the brain, where higher thinking that controls moral reasoning takes place.

There is a third explanation for the link as well, lying in the emotional disconnection that psychologists and psychiatrists call *dissociation*. Much has been made of the famous fight-or-flight response to threat. But as Bruce Perry points out, rarely do children have the option of either fighting or fleeing a situation physically, particularly when, as often is the case, the situation is their membership in an abusive family. Perry notes that the fight-or-flight response is mainly observed mostly in male adults, who, when confronted with a stressful threat, can actually choose between fighting or fleeing. Trapped in their home, in a schoolyard, or in a neighborhood, how do children respond?

How Dissociation Works

The most likely option for children is to flee psychologically, that is, to shut down emotionally and disconnect themselves from their feelings *so that they don't have to feel them anymore*. It's a survival strategy that seems to work—in the short run. By cutting off or disowning the feelings that threaten to overwhelm them, children can survive traumatic threats. But at what cost?

John was six years old when his mother was murdered. He knows that because he was there. The day of the killing his stepfather showed up at the door at three o'clock in the morning, hoping to sneak back into the house after having been thrown out the day before by John's mother. The little boy awoke when he heard the kitchen door open, and he got out of bed to see what was happening. He found his stepfather opening the refrigerator to get a can of beer. "Shush," the man said as John appeared in the doorway to the kitchen. "I don't want your mother to hear me." "Welcome back, Daddy Bill," little John said. "Are you supposed to be here?" "It's okay, boy," John's stepfather replied, patting the boy on the head and moving down the hallway to the master bedroom. John stood in the middle of the kitchen, sleepy but hoping for a glass of milk. In a minute Daddy Bill was back in the kitchen, but he looked very angry. At first, John drew back in fear, because he had experienced his stepfather's anger before.

But Daddy Bill was not angry with little John this time. "Don't be scared, boy," the man said. "You okay. Now just reach in that drawer there," he continued, "and get me that big knife your mother uses to cut meat." John did as he was told. He reached into the drawer next to him and pulled out the big knife, then handed it over to Daddy Bill, who took it in his hand and disappeared down the hallway toward the master bedroom again. The next thing John heard was shouting and screaming coming from the bedroom. He stood there, frozen to the spot, for five or ten minutes, until he felt the pee running down his leg onto his foot. Then he walked down the hallway to the bedroom and looked in. Years later, he says that what he remembers is the red walls. His stepfather killed John's mother, stabbing her fifteen times.

"How did you feel?" I ask him, now two decades later. "I don't remember," he says. "I suppose scared, but I would be lying to you if I said I really remember anything but giving Daddy Bill the knife, hearing the screaming and the shouting, and seeing the red walls." He remembers the events, but he has no memory of the feelings. Poor little boy. As I talk with him, he sits on death row, awaiting execution for stabbing to death a fifty-year-old woman in her bedroom. "How did you feel when you killed that woman?" I ask. "I don't remember," he replies.

Emotional dissociation becomes a hard habit to break. It becomes generalized, giving others the impression that a boy has *no* feelings. In fact the reverse is true: his feelings are so powerful that they must be put in a box and pushed aside to ensure his survival. When incarcerated boys talk about their lives and sometimes their crimes they often seem emotionless. But I know it's not that they don't have feelings; their feelings are locked up inside the young child they have banished for his own protection.

This is emotional territory that is familiar to most males. Boys are routinely taught to ignore or deny their feelings by parents and others who are training them to be men in a culture that demands male stoicism. It is no secret that boys and men in many societies, including our own, are encouraged to put their emotions in boxes, to keep them out of consciousness, and to regard the expression of powerful feelings of pain and sorrow as a highly dangerous activity. We call this compartmentalization, and it is dissociation's first cousin.

CHAPTER 3

Cultural and Political Perspectives on Child Abuse

Chapter Preface

The articles in this chapter reflect changing cultural trends as well as the changing meanings American society places on physical and sexual child abuse. Until the late seventeenth century, not much discussion existed on the nature of childhood or how best to raise and educate children. In the eighteenth and nineteenth centuries in America and Europe, the child-rearing ideas of British philosopher John Locke (1632–1704) gained credence among the educated classes in America. Locke argued that children (and indeed humans) were rational creatures who could learn to want to be good; he argued that corporal punishment only taught children to resent the punisher and bully others, and therefore he only recommended corporal punishment as a "last resort." He recommended that parents withhold affection when children disobey and praise them when they are good. While corporal punishment remained common in the homes of the general public, educated people embraced his ideas, and starting in the nineteenth century, flogging (public whipping) was abolished in the U.S. Navy and regulated or limited in northern schools and orphanages due to the efforts of educators such as Horace Mann.

Prior to the Civil War, child rearing became an increasingly feminine occupation, with fathers working outside the home for long hours and mothers taking on more of the child-rearing responsibility. What is known as the Second Great Awakening (a religious revival lasting from the 1800s through the 1830s), led many Protestants to question how best to manifest their religious beliefs in the world and how best to raise children as Christians. Writers of child-rearing literature popularized the ideas of John Locke, including the rational nature of children who must learn to *want* to be good and the ineffectiveness of corporal punishment in helping children internalize the desire to behave appropriately. The writers of these manuals, from conservative Theodore Dwight, a Calvinist minister, to the more liberal author of children's books, Lydia Maria Child, all emphasize the importance of parental consistency whether a parent chooses to use corporal punishment or not.

How people raise children and what they think constitutes abuse is influenced by their cultural and religious beliefs and religious practices. This chapter introduces the ideas of the seventeenth-century philosopher John Locke and nineteenth-century Calvinist minister Theodore Dwight and then examines the definitions and prevalence of abuse among different religious groups in twentieth-century America.

What people worry about often reflects larger cultural anxieties. This chapter also examines three child abuse "scandals" of the twentieth century that captured the attention of the media and the public. While child neglect is by far the most pernicious form of child abuse in the United States, child sexual abuse gets the most press by far. Each of these child sexual abuse scandals—the day-care sex abuse scandals of the 1980s, the recovered memory controversy of the 1990s, and the Catholic Church sex abuse scandal of the 2000s—is about the sexual abuse of children but also reflects cultural concerns about women entering the workforce and placing children with "strangers" in day care, the public discussion of what had hitherto been private—child sexual abuse in the family—as well as a discussion about what constitutes appropriate and responsible therapy, and repeated abuse of trust by a religious organization as well as the Catholic laity's demand for more transparency and greater participation in church matters.

Whipping Children Does More Harm than Good

John Locke

Influential seventeenth-century philosopher John Locke (1632–1704) had strongly held beliefs that people should not be controlled by authoritarianism or tyranny. In contrast to his contemporary, philosopher Thomas Hobbes (1588–1679), who believed that life was "nasty, brutish and short" and that people were naturally inclined toward short-sighted self-interest, Locke believed that people were inherently rational and that they should to seek truth rather than simply accept the rules handed down by those in authority such as the government, church, teachers, or parents. In his book Some Thoughts Concerning Education, *which he wrote in 1693, Locke questions prevailing ideas about the physical disciplining of children. He suggests that although imposing authority on children by using violent methods such as whipping may create short-term obedience, it also teaches children to bully and to treat others with disrespect to get compliance. Teachers and parents will have better long-term results, he argues, if they encourage children to determine for themselves why it is better to behave and treat others with respect.*

I have spoken so much of carrying a strict hand over children, that perhaps I shall be suspected of not considering enough what is due to their tender age and constitutions. But that opinion will vanish, when you have heard me a little farther. For I am very apt to think, that great severity of punishment does but very little good; nay, great harm in education: and I believe it will be found, that, cæteris paribus [other things being equal] those children who have been most chas-

John Locke, "Some Thoughts Concerning Education." London: Printed for A. J. Churchill, Black Swan, 1693.

tised, seldom make the best men. All that I have hitherto contended for, is, that whatsoever rigour is necessary, it is more to be used, the younger children are; and, having by a due application wrought its effect, it is to be relaxed, and changed into a milder sort of government.

Establish Compliance Early

A compliance, and suppleness of their wills, being by a steady hand introduced by parents, before children have memories to retain the beginnings of it, will seem natural to them, and work afterwards in them, as if it were so; preventing all occasions of struggling, or repining. The only care is, that it be begun early, and inflexibly kept to, till awe and respect be grown familiar, and there appears not the least reluctancy in the submission and ready obedience of their minds. When this reverence is once thus established, (which it must be early, or else it will cost pains and blows to recover it, and the more, the longer it is deferred) it is by it, mixed still with as much indulgence as they made not an ill use of, and not by beating, chiding, or other servile punishments, they are for the future to be governed, as they grow up to more understanding.

That this is so, will be easily allowed, when it is but considered what is to be aimed at, in an ingenuous education; and upon what it turns.

He that has not a mastery over his inclinations, he that knows not how to resist the importunity of present pleasure or pain, for the sake of what reason tells him is fit to be done, wants the true principle of virtue and industry; and is in danger of never being good for any thing. This temper, therefore, so contrary to unguided nature, is to be got betimes; and this habit, as the true foundation of future ability and happiness, is to be wrought into the mind, as early as may be, even from the first dawnings of any knowledge or apprehension in children; and so to be confirmed in them, by all the care and ways imaginable, by those who have the oversight of their education.

On the other side, if the mind be curbed, and humbled too much in children; if their spirits be abased and broken much, by too strict an hand over them; they lose all their vigour and industry, and are in a worse state than the former. For extravagant young fellows, that have liveliness and spirit, come sometimes to be set right, and so make able and great men: but dejected minds, timorous and tame, and low spirits, are hardly ever to be raised, and very seldom attain to any thing. To avoid the danger that is on either hand is the great art: and he that has found a way how to keep up a child's spirit, easy, active, and free; and yet, at the same time, to restrain him from many things he has a mind to, and to draw him to things that are uneasy to him; he, I say, that knows how to reconcile these seeming contradictions, has, in my opinion, got the true secret of education.

The Rod Is an Ineffective Shortcut to Discipline

The usual lazy and short way by chastisement, and the rod, which is the only instrument of government that tutors generally know, or ever think of, is the most unfit of any to be used in education; because it tends to both those mischiefs; which, as we have shown, are the Scylla and Charybdis [dangers on either side of a narrow path, requiring one to be careful], which, on the one hand or the other, ruin all that miscarry.

This kind of punishment contributes not at all to the mastery of our natural propensity to indulge corporal and present pleasure, and to avoid pain at any rate; but rather encourages it; and thereby strengthens that in us, which is the root, from whence spring all vicious actions and the irregularities of life. From what other motive, but of sensual pleasure, and pain, does a child act, who drudges at his book against his inclination, or abstains from eating unwholesome fruit, that he takes pleasure in, only out of fear of whipping? He in this only prefers the greater corporal pleasure, or avoids the greater corporal pain. And what is it to govern his actions, and direct his conduct, by such motives as these? what is it, I say, but to cherish that principle in him, which it is our business to root out and destroy? And therefore I cannot think any correction useful to a child, where the shame of suffering for having done amiss does not work more upon him than the pain.

Beating Encourages Dishonesty and Fear

This sort of correction naturally breeds an aversion to that which it is the tutor's business to create a liking to. How obvious is it to observe, that children come to hate things which were at first acceptable to them, when they find themselves whipped, and chid [scolded], and teazed about them? And it is not to be wondered at in them; when grown men would not be able to be reconciled to any thing by such ways. Who is there that would not be disgusted with any innocent recreation, in itself indifferent to him, if he should with blows, or ill language, be hauled to it, when he had no mind? or be constantly so treated, for some circumstances in his application to it? This is natural to be so. Offensive circumstances ordinarily infect innocent things, which they are joined with: and the very sight of a cup, wherein any one uses to take nauseous physic, turns his stomach; so that nothing will relish well out of it, though the cup be ever so clean, and well-shaped, and of the richest materials.

Such a sort of slavish [slavelike] discipline makes a slavish temper. The child submits, and dissembles obedience, whilst the fear of the rod hangs over him; but when that is removed, and, by being out of sight, he can promise himself impunity, he gives the greater scope to his natural inclination; which by this way is not at all altered, but on the contrary heightened and increased in him; and after such restraint, breaks out usually with the more violence. Or,

If severity carried to the highest pitch does prevail, and works a cure upon the present unruly distemper, it is often bringing in the room of it worse and more dangerous disease, by breaking the mind; and then, in the place of a disorderly young fellow, you have a low-spirited moped creature: who, however with his unnatural sobriety he may please silly people, who commend tame inactive children, because they make no noise, nor give them any trouble; yet, at last, will probably prove as uncomfortable a thing to his friends, as he will be, all his life, an useless thing to himself and others.

Avoid Bribery and Flattery

Beating then, and all other sorts of slavish and corporal punishments, are not the discipline fit to be used in the education of those who would have wise, good, and ingenuous men; and therefore very rarely to be applied, and that only on great occasions, and cases of extremity. On the other side, to flatter children by rewards of things that are pleasant to them, is as carefully to be avoided. He that will give to his son apples, or sugar-plums, or what else of this kind he is most delighted with, to make him learn his book, does but authorise his love of pleasure, and cocker up [indulge] that dangerous propensity, which he ought by all means to subdue and stifle in him. You can never hope to teach him to master it, whilst you compound for the check you give his inclination in one place, by the satisfaction you propose to it in another. To make a good, a wise, and a virtuous man, it is fit he should learn to cross his appetite, and deny his inclination to riches, finery, or pleasing his palate, &c. whenever his reason advises the contrary, and his duty requires it. But when you draw him to do any thing that is fit, by the offer of money; or reward the pains of learning his book, by the pleasure of a luscious morsel; when you promise him a lace-cravat, or a fine new suit, upon performance of some of his little tasks; what do you, by proposing these as rewards, but allow them to be the good things he should aim at, and thereby encourage his longing for them, and accustom him to place his happiness in them? Thus people, to prevail with children to be industrious about their grammar, dancing, or some other such matter, of no great moment to the happiness or usefulness of their lives, by misapplied rewards and punishments, sacrifice their virtue, invert the order of their education, and teach them luxury, pride, or covetousness, &c. For in this way, flattering those wrong inclinations, which they should restrain and suppress, they lay the foundations of those future vices, which cannot be avoided, but by curbing our desires, and accustoming them early to submit to reason.

Treat Children As Rational Creatures

But if you take away the rod on one hand, and these little encouragements, which they are taken with, on the other; how then (will you say) shall children be governed? Remove hope and fear, and there is an end of all discipline. I grant, that good and evil, reward and punishment, are the only motives to a rational creature; these are the spur and reins, whereby all mankind are set on work and guided, and therefore they are to be made use of to children too. For I advise their parents and governors always to carry this in their minds, that children are to be treated as rational creatures.

The rewards and punishments then whereby we should keep children in order are quite of another kind; and of that force, that when we can get them once to work, the business, I think, is done, and the difficulty is over. Esteem and disgrace are, of all others, the most powerful incentives to the mind, when once it is brought to relish them. If you can once get into children a love of credit, and an apprehension of shame and disgrace, you have put into them the true principle, which will constantly work, and incline them to the right. But it will be asked, How shall this be done?

I confess, it does not, at first appearance, want some difficulty; but yet I think it worth our while to seek the ways (and practise them when found) to attain this, which I look on as the great secret of education.

Praise, Good Behavior, Shame, Bad Behavior

First, children (earlier perhaps than we think) are very sensible of praise and commendation. They find a pleasure in being esteemed and valued, especially by their parents, and those whom they depend on. If therefore the father caress and commend them, when they do well; show a cold and neglectful countenance to them upon doing ill; and this accompanied by a like carriage of the mother, and all others that are about them; it will in a little time make them sensible of the difference: and this, if constantly observed, I doubt not but will of itself work more than threats or blows, which lose their force, when once grown common, and are of no use when shame does not attend them; and therefore are to be forborn, and never to be used, but in the case hereafter mentioned, when it is brought to extremity.

But, secondly, to make the sense of esteem or disgrace sink the deeper, and be of the more weight, other agreeable or disagreeable things should constantly accompany these different states; not as particular rewards and punishments of this or that particular action, but as necessarily belonging to, and constantly attending one, who by his carriage has brought himself into a state of disgrace or commendation. By which way of treating them, children may as much as possible be brought to conceive, that those that are commended and in esteem for doing well, will necessarily be beloved and cherished by every body, and have all other good things as a consequence of it; and, on the other side, when any one by miscarriage falls into dis-esteem, and cares not to preserve his credit, he will unavoidably fall under neglect and contempt: and, in that state, the want of whatever might satisfy or delight him, will follow. In this way the objects of their desires are made assisting to virtue; when a settled experience from the beginning teaches children, that the things they delight in, belong to, and are to enjoyed by those only, who are in a state of reputation. If by these means you can come once to shame them out of their faults, (for besides that, I would willingly have no punishment) and make them in love with the pleasure of being well thought on, you may turn them as you please, and they will be in love with all the ways of virtue....

Frequent Beatings Are Not Effective

Frequent beating or chiding is therefore carefully to be avoided; because this sort of correction never produces any good, farther than it serves to raise shame and abhorrence of the miscarriage that brought it on them. And if the greatest part of the trouble be not the sense that they have done amiss, and the apprehension that they have drawn on themselves the just displeasure of their best friends, the pain of whipping will work but an imperfect cure. It only patches up for the present, and skins it over, but reaches not to the bottom of the sore. Ingenuous shame, and the apprehension of displeasure, are the only true restraints: these alone ought to hold the reins, and keep the child in order. But corporal punishments must necessarily lose that effect, and wear out the sense of shame, where they frequently return. Shame in children has the same place that modesty has in women; which cannot be kept, and often transgressed against. And as to the apprehension of displeasure in the parents, they will come to be very insignificant, if the marks of that displeasure quickly cease, and a few blows fully expiate. Parents should well consider, what faults in their children are weighty enough to deserve the declaration of their anger: but when their displeasure is once declared to a degree that carries any punishment with it, they ought not presently to lay by the severity of their brows, but to restore their children to their former grace with some difficulty; and delay a full reconciliation, till their conformity, and more than ordinary merit, make good their amendment. If this be not so ordered, punishment will, by familiarity, become a mere thing of course, and lose all its influence: offending, being chastised, and then forgiven, will be thought as natural and necessary as noon, night, and morning, following one another.

Corporal Punishment Can Be Part of Christian Discipline

Theodore Dwight Jr.

From 1800 to the 1830s, the American people were caught up in a religious revival movement called the Second Great Awakening, which encouraged them to reform their world. Fueled by a desire to lead Christian lives, activists questioned slavery, poverty, and economic inequality, as well as children's and women's rights. The following treatise by Theodore Dwight Jr. (1796–1866), a congressman and Calvinist minister, is representative of conservative Christian beliefs on child rearing in early nineteenth-century America. In his book The Father's Book, *Dwight suggests that, while corporal punishment should be used sparingly with disobedient children, there are times, he believes, when whipping is necessary to maintain discipline. Dwight is in good company. In* The Mother's Book *(1831), Lydia Maria Child, a novelist and progress reformer, also maintains that when more gentle forms of punishment have failed to make a child behave, whipping is an acceptable last resort. Both authors emphasize the importance of parental consistency, so that children do not experience punishment as capricious, that is, based on their parents' whims or moods.*

With respect to the government or discipline of a family, some important points are to be regarded. Almost every other plan will be thwarted if there is not a proper submission to authority. And this will not be secured where it is not properly exercised. This cannot be said to be done where children are treated as if they were different beings from what they are. Some parents err by presuming that their children know less, or more, than they do; or have worse or better dis-

Theodore Dwight Jr., "Family Government," *The Father's Book; Or, Suggestions for the Government and Instruction of Young Children on Principles Appropriate to a Christian Country.* Springfield: G. & C. Merriam, 1834, pp. 108–117.

positions than they have; or less or more command over their minds or feelings. Some place too much reliance on force, others on kindness; some change their plans frequently, others have no plans at all, but notice or pass over faults, blame and approve, according to their own feelings at the moment. Many unteach by example faster than they instruct by precept. . . .

Corporal Punishment Is a Scriptural Duty

Corporal punishments, as most parents will allow, should be but seldom inflicted. While their efficacy has been overrated by many, and underrated by some, they are undoubtedly often made worse than none at all; and yet they are capable of being used, in particular cases and in a proper manner, with good results, when other means have failed. The Scriptures represent punishment as a strange work to our Heavenly Father. Every judicious parent will endeavor to render punishment of any kind unnecessary; but yet will not shrink from administering it when duty imperiously requires. A vast number of punishments of all kinds might have been spared to children, by proper attention in consulting their wants and comforts; and many which have been injudiciously applied, had better never have been resorted to.

Children Must Be Taught to Discipline Themselves

A young child should not be punished for every fretful expression. Soothing words, an embrace, a new and pleasant object of attention, will often suppress rising irritability; and against the first appearances of evil the parents should be ever watchful. These are the young shoots of disaffection, anger, hatred, violence, disobedience, profanity and murder, and should be suppressed as early as possible. Some parents seem to think, that the evil passions are most effectually destroyed, by exciting them in their children, or allowing them to proceed to a great length, and then applying some severe punishment. It would be far better, if we could keep the young from ever experiencing these violent emotions, and habituate them to quench the first stirrings of bad temper. The child must be his own chief disciplinarian through life, and the art of self-government must be taught him, as a regular part of his education, and that both by precept and example. Not a hasty expression, not a step, nor a motion, nor a look, ought ever to be seen in the parent, indicative of passion. The constant study of a model of self-possession in a father, or a mother, will do more to control the temper of a child, than any series of punishments.

Willful Disobedience

Every instance of disobedience should not be punished though every wilful refusal to obey a parent should be. I can give my views on this point best in the language of a highly respected friend. "I once thought," said he, "that instantaneous obedience should be required of my children: but I found that the little ones could not be brought in every instance to comply at once with my commands. If I say 'pick up that key,' to a child of three or four, while engaged with something else, it will often stand and look at me: 'pick up that key'—it stands still—'pick up that key'—the third or fourth time, it may be, I am obeyed. Now is this wilful disobedience? The child looks at me, from first to last, without passion, and perhaps even with smiles and confidence. No—I think rather that its mind is occupied with another subject, and does not readily change it. Besides, a child is sometimes unable to discover, whether the parent is in earnest or in sport, and its own feelings strongly incline it to the latter. If, however, after time has been given for it to fix its attention, and to perceive that I am in earnest, it proves stubborn and resolute in disobedience, I calmly warn it against the evil spirit that is rising, its tendency, the offence against God and myself, and the punishment that must follow; and last of all comes the punishment. With an older child I should make less allowance, especially if I had trained it properly before."

Gentle Discipline Is More Effective than Harsh Punishment

The most harsh punishments are not of course the most effectual—often quite the contrary. A child, gently trained by a gentle parent, receives the most poignant wounds through the heart. I have seen a slight expression of disapprobation from such a parent produce a flood of tears in a young child; and many instances are on record, in which the mild reproof or the silent tear of a good parent, has pierced the feelings of much older children. The love of his parent and his Maker should be the leading strings of a child, and the fear of losing it a sufficient motive to deter them from evil. When these fail, however, as they often will, especially while parents are far from perfection in exercising government, punishments must be resorted to, and gratifications must be denied; as by the removal of playthings, confinement to a corner, to a room, or in fine weather, to the house, temporary banishment from the table, or the society of playmates. These, and the denial of instruction on some interesting subject, may be resorted to, and should be successively tried, with well-timed expostulations, and friendly exhortations to struggle against the evil propensity. The child should be taught that all persons have wrong feelings by nature, but that they may be overcome, with great exertion, and the help of God; that the parent has thus overcome them, and that such and such good people have resorted to such and such means with success. Every favorable opportunity should be taken to read to the child in the Scriptures, to pray with it, and induce it to pray for itself; and the knowledge that it is ardently and affectionately prayed for, will be very likely to melt it into penitence. After the feelings have been soothed by means like these, even if the temper be not entirely subdued, it may be well sometimes to allow the child to retire, and engage in some tranquillizing employment; or to fall asleep, which will probably restore that self-control which he has perhaps hardly strength to exercise after this agitation.

Nothing should be used as a punishment which a child ought to like, or ought readily submit to in other circumstances. "If you do not say your prayers," a mother was heard to say to her little daughter one evening in a steamboat, "you shall take a dose of castor oil and salts!" Many parents injudiciously shut children in dark or lonely places, when they have superstitious fears, or are likely to have them. Such remedies are worse than almost any disease; I mean, a resort to them is more dangerous, than the neglect to punish common offences.

Corporal Punishment Can Lose Effect

Corporal punishments are sometimes necessary, but they lose their effect by frequent application and at the same time deaden those feelings which should be fostered. They should produce short but real pain. A blow with the hand upon a child's head may stupify without stinging, and may produce lasting injury. The bones are tender and small, and a light rod is safer than the hand. Whether corporal punishments should be inflicted on the spot, or after some delay, has been debated. They should never be inflicted by a person in a passion. I have heard of a child of three, corrected with much apparent effect, after a lapse of some hours, an admonition and a prayer, with acquiescence on its own part, because it had done what such punishment had been threatened for. I would however seldom threaten such whipping; for in such a case it might have been dispensed with but for the threat. The long anticipation of such punishment increases its severity many fold; so that it may thus become greatly disproportioned to the offence. When however the offence has been very aggravated, such an enhancement of it may be most judicious.

Children should be obedient—must be obedient, habitually and cheerfully so, or they cannot be well educated in any respect.

Habits of truth and honesty, of reverence for parents, the aged, and especially for the Almighty, should be most sedulously cultivated, and insisted upon. Any plain violation of such rules should be noticed and dwelt upon as a thing of great moment—an offence not to be overlooked or slighted. The child should understand, by the earnestness and serious displeasure of the parent, that such practices are not to be tolerated, but perseveringly rooted out, under a solemn sense of duty to God.

Religious Affiliation Influences What Parents Believe About Corporal Punishment

Denise A. Hines and Kathleen Malley-Morrison

Denise A. Hines is a postdoctoral research fellow at the Family Research Laboratory and Crimes Against Children Research Center at the University of New Hampshire with Murray Straus and David Finkelhor, who are leaders in the field of family violence. Kathleen Malley-Morrison is a professor of psychology at Boston University and has conducted extensive research on family violence. Malley-Morrison is particularly interested in cross-cultural and international perspectives on family violence. In this excerpt from Family Violence in the United States, *Hines and Malley-Morrison describe how religious differences can influence child-rearing practices and what is considered abusive parenting. They focus on the core values of different religious groups in the United States as well as on the prevalence of physical abuse, sexual abuse, and neglect across those groups.*

Much of the limited research on cultural values concerning child rearing and child discipline within different religions has focused on the values and beliefs of conservative Protestants as compared with other groups. Conservative Protestants have a distinct set of cultural values supportive of corporal punishment encapsulated in many of their child-rearing manuals. An analysis of best-selling conservative and mainstream Protestant child-rearing manuals revealed that mainstream Protestant manuals emphasized democratic parent-child relationships and open communication between parents and children, while conservative Protestant manuals empha-

Denise A. Hines and Kathleen Malley-Morrison, *Family Violence in the United States: Defining, Understanding, and Combating Abuse.* Thousand Oaks, CA: Sage Publications, 2005, pp. 63–70. Copyright © 2005 by Sage Publications, Inc. All rights reserved. Reproduced by permission of Sage Publications, Inc.

sized obedience and submission. Whereas mainstream manuals emphasized the parental use of reasoning tactics, conservative manuals emphasized corporal punishment. In particular, the conservative manuals recommended that parents use a rod to administer physical punishment to children whenever children show willful defiance to parental authority. . . .

It is somewhat difficult to obtain a clear picture of differences between religious groups in both endorsement and use of corporal punishment and in frequency of child abuse reports for several reasons: (1) various investigators have classified religions differently and grouped them together in different ways; (2) lumping together different Protestant denominations in order to compare Protestants and Catholics, as has been done in some studies, ignores the wide range of values characterizing the different Protestant denominations; (3) measures of constructs such as religiosity and religious conservatism have varied considerably across studies; and (4) variables such as geography, ethnicity, and social class tend to be confounded with affiliation.

Despite these limitations, some important findings have emerged. National survey data support the propositions that there are differences between religions in support for corporal punishment, and the endorsement of particular religious beliefs (e.g., that the Bible is the literal word of God) is positively associated with convictions concerning corporal punishment. For example, the first wave of the National Survey of Families and Households (NSFH) revealed that Jewish parents were significantly less likely than Protestant or Catholic parents, and Protestant parents were more likely than parents with no religious affiliation, to use corporal punishment. According to the 1990 National Longitudinal Study of Youth, Catholics had the lowest use of spanking of all the groups studied. In a more localized study of couples in a southwestern city, conservative Protestant parents spanked their children more often than mainline Protestant, Roman Catholic, and unaffiliated parents. Moreover, 29% of the conservative Protestant parents said they spanked their children three or more times a week, as compared to only 3% of Roman Catholic and none of the unaffiliated parents. Whereas the conservative Protestants emphasized the instrumental benefits of spanking, the mainline Protestants and Roman Catholics anticipated more negative effects of spanking. Mainline Protestant and unaffiliated parents were more likely to indicate they would try to reason with their children about misbehavior than conservative Protestants.

Two smaller religious denominations of particular interest to researchers are Quakers (because of their advocacy of nonviolence) and Mormons (because of their strict patriarchal traditions). A survey of nearly 300 Quakers revealed that 75% of mothers and 69% of fathers reported violence toward their children. As compared to national norms, Quaker mothers and fathers reported more kicking, biting, and punching of their children, all of which are typically considered to be abusive in mainstream society. Interestingly, Quaker parents reported less slapping and hitting with objects, which may be the most normative forms of corporal punishment among Protestants in general. In contrast to the national sample, where some fathers reported beating their children and threatening or using guns or knives on their children, no Quaker fathers reported these forms of violence against their children. Thus, even though Quakers advocate nonviolence, it does not necessarily mean that they do not physically punish their children; they may just use different forms of physical punishment than the majority culture. In a study of Mormons, rates of severe child physical abuse were slightly lower in a Utah sample (80% Mormon) than the rates in the U.S. as a whole (9.3% versus 10.7%). Thus, rates of child maltreatment in Mormons appear to be the same or slightly less than nationwide rates, even though the patriarchal structure of their religion would lead some to theorize that they would be more likely to physically punish their children.

Despite considerable differences among congregational communities within religions in their values relating to the use of aggression in families, there has been very little research comparing the smaller Christian and non-Christian denominations and sects on their values and practices. In a rare comparative study, Malley-Morrison and Hines (2003) found, in a convenience sample of nearly 500 people, that Christians, as a group, reported having experienced significantly more corporal punishment than Jews, Hindus, and atheists/ agnostics. When comparisons were made among principal denominational groupings, they found that Presbyterians tended to be somewhat less tolerant of corporal punishment than both conservative Protestants and Catholics. Jews had experienced less corporal punishment as children, and were also somewhat less tolerant of it, than conservative Protestants. Conservative Jews were more tolerant of corporal punishment than Reformed Jews. Finally, the agnostic/atheist group had experienced less corporal punishment than the Catholics but were more supportive of parental use of corporal punishment than Buddhists, Reformed Jews, and Conservative Jews.

Although denominational differences have been found, the espousal of particular religious beliefs may be a more important predictor of aggression in families than simple religious affiliation. In the NSFH, degree of endorsement of items such as, "I regard myself as a religious fundamentalist," was significantly positively correlated with parents' likelihood of using corporal punishment. An analysis of parents' reported use of physical punishment to discipline preschool and elementary school-aged children showed that parents who believed the Bible is the inerrant Word of God and provides answers to all human problems used corporal punishment more frequently than parents with less conservative theological views. The national General Social Survey of 1988 had similar findings:

Conservative Protestants were significantly more supportive of corporal punishment than members of other religious groups. Endorsement of the items, "Human nature is fundamentally perverse and corrupt," and, "Those who violate God's rules must be punished," was the strongest predictor of tolerance of corporal punishment.

Other studies confirm the finding that a conservative world view may contribute more to approval of corporal punishment than religion or religiosity. A 1995 national Gallup Poll revealed that parents who were more conservative in their social ideologies had more positive attitudes toward physical discipline. In a random sample from Oklahoma City, even after accounting for socioeconomic and demographic variables, belief in the literalness of the Bible accounted for a large share of the differences between religious groups in degree of advocacy of corporal punishment. Similarly, among Protestants from five central and southern states, both males and females who believed in a literal interpretation of the Bible showed greater endorsement of statements such as, "Children should always be spanked when they misbehave," and "Parents spoil their children by picking them up and comforting them when they cry."

Independent of the issue of whether corporal punishment is abusive, some studies have specifically addressed physical child abuse as a problem that may vary by religion. In the first National Family Violence Survey, the rate of child abuse was lowest among Jews and highest in families where one or both parents had a "minority religious affiliation." The lower rates of family violence among Jews may be related to their generally higher levels of income, education, and employment. Conversely, members of minority religions may experience more discrimination, stress, and isolation from mainstream society, characteristics that may lead to greater violence within their homes. . . .

Child Sexual Abuse

There is little research with representative samples to provide reliable estimates of the prevalence of intrafamilial sexual abuse in different religious groups. Of nearly 1,000 women living in the San Francisco area, the following percentages of women reported having experienced childhood sexual abuse: approximately 43% of Protestants, 37% of Jews, 37% of Catholics, and 30% of those with other affiliations; there were no significant differences in prevalence, and no breakdown was given for intrafamilial versus extrafamilial abuse. A survey of nearly 3,000 professional women from across the United States presented a somewhat different picture: approximately 39% of women with agnostic/atheistic parents, 32% with families of some religion other than conservative Christianity, and 18% from conservative Christian families reported some form of childhood sexual abuse (either intra- or extrafamilial). More specifically, women raised in conservative Christian homes where there was little emphasis on incorporating religious values into family life (i.e., low intrinsic religiosity) reported significantly higher rates of sexual abuse than women raised in Christian homes with higher integration of religious values (i.e., high intrinsic religiosity) or women raised in nonconservative Christian homes. Elliott speculated that conservative Christians who do not integrate their professed beliefs into their lifestyles may use those doctrines primarily to justify their own controlling tactics with family members and intimidate their victims into silence.

Although incest is prohibited by both Hebrew and Christian scripture, it is clear that it occurs in many homes—including conservative Protestant homes. In one study of 35 women who had been sexually abused in childhood in their conservative Protestant homes, the mean age of the girls when the incest began was just under six years, with a range from 2 to 16 years; 37% of the women had been preschoolers when the sexual abuse started. The abusers were fathers in 66% of the cases and stepfathers in 34% of the cases. The natural fathers were evenly distributed across the denominational categories (including Presbyterians, Methodists, Lutherans, Baptists, and Fundamentalists who espoused conservative Christian values); however, 82% of the abusive stepfathers were Fundamentalists. The natural fathers were more likely to perpetrate the more serious forms of sexual abuse (e.g., involving penetration) than the stepfathers. . . .

Child Neglect

A major form of religion-related child abuse identified by a national sample of mental health professionals is the withholding of medical care for religious reasons. Approximately 10% of neglect cases identified by professionals involved this form of neglect. Most of the parents in these cases were classified as "fundamentalist" (e.g., Mormon, Pentecostal, Seventh Day Adventist). Among fundamentalists, a number of different religious beliefs lead to resistance against certain forms of medical care. For example, Jehovah's Witnesses believe that the Bible prohibits blood transfusions and therefore any procedures necessitating a transfusion. Christian Scientists believe that sickness and pain are errors of the mortal mind, all diseases are mental conditions, and healing the sick must involve driving out misperceptions rather than using procedures like medications, which only relieve suffering temporarily but do not cure the problem. The principal exception to the Christian Science system is the use of medical care in childbirth and to set broken bones.

Consider the case of *In re Sampson*, in which the court was asked to intervene on behalf of a 15-year-old boy with a serious facial deformity resulting from a medical condition called neurofibromatosis. Because of this condition, the boy was extremely emotionally withdrawn, would not attend school, and was virtually illiterate. Although his condition was not life-threatening, his physicians indicated that they could improve his appearance surgically. Because the procedure would involve considerable medical risk, they were unwilling to undertake the procedure without authorization to provide blood transfusions if necessary. The mother, a Jehovah's Witness, refused to agree to the surgery if there was a chance that it would require a transfusion. Is the mother's refusal in this case to allow her son to have the corrective surgery a type of neglect, some other form of maltreatment, or appropriate parenting within the context of her religion? If you were the judge considering the physicians' argument that surgery would benefit the boy, what would your conclusion be? In this case, the court decided the boy was a neglected minor and ordered his mother to permit the surgery and to consent to a transfusion if the doctors decided it was necessary during the course of treatment. . . .

The debate over parental failure to obtain medical care for their children for religious reasons has generally been one of balancing the children's medical needs with parental rights to rear children in accordance with their religious beliefs. The issue becomes more complex when we consider childhood immunizations, which involve not just the well-being of the individual child but the well-being of the community. If fundamentalist families objecting to immunizations are concentrated in fairly large communities, any refusal to allow immunizations has the potential for creating a rather serious public health risk for the whole community. The American Academy of Pediatrics has taken the position that, "Constitutional guarantees of freedom of religion do not permit children to be harmed through religious practices, nor do they allow religion to be a valid legal defense when an individual harms or neglects a child."

Epidemic or Hysteria?
Day Care Sex Abuse Scandals
in the 1980s

Mary de Young

In 1983 the operators of California's McMartin Preschool were accused of subjecting the children in their care to horrific abuse, including satanic rituals. This led to a lengthy investigation and trial, as well as accusations of abuse at other schools and day-care centers across the country in subsequent years. Ultimately, none of the charges in the McMartin case were substantiated. Sociologist Mary de Young considers the day-care scandals part of a "moral panic" that resulted from cultural anxieties over women working outside the home and entrusting child care to professionals. As a result of the day-care scandals, clinicians and law enforcement personnel who interview children about abuse must follow an appropriate protocol that uses open-ended questioning and avoids "leading" children to any particular answer. Additionally, since the 1980s, statewide oversight of day-care centers has vastly improved; day-care centers must now be licensed, and day-care providers are screened for criminal and psychiatric histories.

[T]he McMartin Preschool of Manhattan Beach, California,] founded in 1956 by Virginia Steely McMartin ... had a certain cachet among local residents and a six month waiting list. . . .

The day-to-day administration of the preschool was left to her 55 year old daughter, Peggy McMartin Buckey, a garrulous former dancer and social gadfly. It was her husband, Charles,

Mary de Young, "The Devil Goes To Day Care," *The Day Care Ritual Abuse Moral Panic.* Jefferson, NC: McFarland & Company, Inc., 2004, pp. 26–42. Copyright © 2004 Mary de Young. All rights reserved. Reproduced by permission of McFarland & Company, Inc., Box 611, Jefferson NC 28640. www.mcfarlandpub.com.

who had built the whimsical child-sized wooden animals that dotted the preschool yard that also featured a wooden car, a jungle gym, a fort and a playhouse *sans* doors. Peggy's daughter, Peggy Ann, 28, occasionally taught at the preschool when she could take time from her job as a teacher for the hearing impaired in the Anaheim Union public schools. Her 25 year old son Raymond, a lanky, lantern-jawed college dropout also taught at the preschool, attracted to this traditionally defined "women's work" by the opportunity to work with children, whom he considered "more honest than adults.". . .

[In 1983] Judy Johnson, recently separated from her husband, drinking heavily, and raising their two young sons alone, left her two-and-a-half year old in the yard of the preschool. Taking pity on the woebegone child whose name they found on a slip of paper in his pocket, the providers took him in. Over the next few months, he attended the McMartin Preschool fourteen times.

Charges of Molestation

In August, Judy Johnson called the local police to accuse Raymond Buckey of molesting her son. The boy had come from the preschool with a reddened anus and had spent the night restless and whiny, finally responding to his mother's relentless questioning by saying that Buckey had taken his temperature rectally. Assuming the "thermometer" her son described actually was Buckey's penis, she concluded that he had been sodomized by the only male provider at the preschool.

The medical exam conducted the next day was inconclusive for sodomy, however, and the boy disclosed nothing to an investigating detective. But the matter was far from over. Johnson began calling other parents of the preschool enrollees, asking them to question their children. None confirmed the stories her son allegedly was telling her—the stories about sexual abuse, bondage and nude photographs that she was passing on to the police in almost daily telephone calls. The police, in turn, requested another medical exam of her son. This one was conducted by an inexperienced intern who, convinced by the allegations Johnson made on her silent son's behalf, diagnosed anal penetration and referred mother and son to a local counseling center.

The ensuing police investigation was deeply unsettling for Buckey whose reputation as a loner and ne'er-do-well was quite well known to the parents of the preschool enrollees. After searching the home he lived in with his parents, Buckey was arrested and then quietly released for lack of evidence. Persisting in their investigation, however, the police sent the following letter to two hundred families of children currently or previously enrolled at the preschool:

> Please question your child to see if he or she has been a witness to any crime or if he or she has been a victim. Our investigation indicates that possible criminal acts include oral sex, fondling of genitals, buttocks or chest areas and sodomy, possibly committed under the pretense of "taking the child's temperature." Also, photos may have been taken of the children without their clothing. Any information from your child regarding having ever observed Ray Buckey to leave a classroom alone with a child during any nap period, of if they have ever observed Ray Buckey tie up a child, is important. Please complete the enclosed information form and return it to this department in the enclosed stamped envelope as soon as possible.

A Community in Turmoil

Although the letter also admonished parents not to discuss the investigation with anyone, the same "small town living, friendly neighbors, and community spirit" that made Manhattan Beach a nice place to live also quickly made it a vipers nest of rumors. Parents not only questioned their own children, but interrogated each other during chance meetings in local stores and in frantic late night telephone calls. Only a few children disclosed anything, but some who did embellished the accounts of Judy Johnson who ventriloquially was still speaking for her silent son. While Johnson told police her son disclosed that Buckey had inserted air tubes in his anus, killed a dog, took him home to have oral sex with a stranger, wore clown and minister costumes, and chopped living rabbits into pieces, other children now talked about naked games and sexual abuse of all kinds not only by Buckey, but his grandmother, mother, sister, and the other three providers.

By the fall of 1983 the laid back seaside community of Manhattan Beach was in turmoil. Taking the opportunity to get some political mileage out of the uproar in a county that had cited child abuse as one of its most pressing issues, District Attorney Robert Philibosian assigned one of his assistants, Jean Matusinka, to oversee the case. She, in turn, introduced the anxious parents to the Children's Institute International, a non-profit child abuse diagnostic and treatment facility, where videotaped interviews would be conducted by experts in order to reduce both the number of interviews and interviewers the children would have to encounter.

The expert who would assume the responsibility for conducting most of the interviews was social worker Kee MacFarlane, a former grants reviewer for the National Center for Child Abuse and Neglect. With Jean Matusinka and psychiatrist Roland Summit, she was part of a group discussing the sexual abuse of young children and was eager to test the received wisdom that only persistent and leading questions would break through the "child sexual abuse accommodation syndrome," the interrogative effects of that style of interview softened through the use of hand puppets. MacFarlane had stumbled upon the technique of using hand puppets a year or so before she even became involved in the McMartin Preschool case. "I was talking to a preschooler who was holding a puppet in her hand," she recalls, "and she refused to answer a question. I said, 'Maybe the puppet would like to answer!' And it worked."

It certainly did. By the time she and her colleagues were finished, over 350 of the 400 children interviewed, at a cost to the state of $455 for each interview and medical examination, had made allegations against one or more of the McMartin providers.

Puppet Interviews

The puppets hardly deserve all the credit. It was in interviews that led, begged, bribed, cajoled, shamed and intimidated that the allegations came forth. . . .

In some interviews, children were lavishly praised for confirming the interviewer's bias. Take as an example the approval heaped on one child who, after a series of suggestive questions, finally agreed with the interviewer that a provider had photographed the children while they were naked: "Can I pat you on the head . . .? Look at what a good help you can be. You're going to help all these little children because you're so smart." Yet as facilely as praise was proffered, so was shame, as the following exchange about the "Naked Movie Star Game" that some of the children described as a pretense for taking pornographic pictures of them illustrates:

Interviewer: I thought that was a naked game.

Child: Not exactly.

Interviewer: Did somebody take their clothes off?.

Child: When I was there no one was naked.

Interviewer: We want to make sure you're not scared to tell.

Child: I'm not scared.

Interviewer: Some of the kids were told they might be killed. It was a trick. All right Mr. Alligator [the puppet the child is using], are you going to be stupid, or are you smart and can tell. Some think you're smart.

Child: I'll be smart.

Interviewer: Mr. Monkey [a puppet the child had used earlier] is chicken. He can't remember the naked games, but you know the naked movie star game. Is your memory too bad?

Child: I haven't seen the naked movie star game.

Interviewer: You must be dumb!

Child: I don't remember.

Leading Questions

In a different tactic, some children were badgered not only in making an allegation, but in providing perceptual detail. In this interview a PacMan puppet is used to intimidate an eight year old in describing ejaculate:

Interviewer: Here's a hard question I don't know if you know the answer to. We'll see how smart you are, PacMan. Did you ever see anything come out of Mr. Ray's weiner? Do you remember that?

Child: [No response]

Interviewer: Can you remember back that far? We'll see how . . . how good your brain is working today, PacMan. [Child moves puppet around.] Is that a yes. [Child nods the puppet]. Well, you're smart. Now, let's see if we can figure out what it was. I wonder if you can point to something of what color it was. [Child tries to pick up the pointer with the PacMan's mouth.] Let me get your pen here [puts pointer in PacMan's mouth].

Child: I was. . . .

Interviewer: Let's see what color is that. [Child uses the PacMan's hand to point to the PacMan puppet.] Oh, you're pointing to yourself. That must be yellow. [Child nods puppet yes.] You're smart to point to yourself. What did it feel like? Was it like water? Or something else?

Child: Um, what?

Interviewer: The stuff that came out. Let me try. I'll try a different question on you. We'll try to figure out what that stuff tastes like. We're going to try and figure out if it tastes good.

Child: He never did that to me, I don't think.

Interviewer: Oh, well, PacMan, would you know what it tastes like? Would you think it tastes like candy, sort of trying . . .

Child: I think it would taste like yucky ants.

Interviewer: Yucky ants. Whoa. That would be kind of yucky. I don't think it would taste like . . . you don't think it would taste like strawberries or anything good?

Child: No.

Interviewer: Oh. Think it would so . . . do you think that would be sticky, like sticky, yucky ants?

Child: A little.

Part of the grist for these interviews most certainly came from Judy Johnson who, Cassandra-like, was warning interviewers of what they would hear if only they could work through their own incredulity and listen as well as she was to her own son. In telephone calls and letters Johnson claimed the McMartin providers had stapled his eyes shut, stabbed scissors in his tongue, buried him in a coffin without air holes, and forced him to drink blood. She said he described black candles, witch costumes, Raymond Buckey flying through the air, animal sacrifices, and his providers chopping off a baby's head and burning the brains. . . .

The News Media

A six minute television news story during "sweeps week" in February 1984 gave credence to what was still rumor, suspicion and innuendo. "More than sixty children, some of them as young as two years of age . . . have now told authorities that he or she has been keeping a grotesque secret of being sexually abused and made to appear in pornographic films while in the preschool's care, and of having been forced to witness the mutilation and killing of animals to scare the kids into staying silent," intoned KABC reporter Wayne Satz. "The allegations are being taken very seriously.". . .

Journalistic skepticism was replaced with credulity, critical thinking with mushy emotionality, and objectivity with an ardent belief that the McMartin providers were guilty and could not be proved innocent.

Even the venerable *Los Angeles Times* could not rise above criticism. In a Pulitzer Prize winning series, reporter David Shaw castigates his own newspaper for minimizing or ignoring completely stories that would have called into question the allegations against the McMartin providers, and for pandering to the growing community hysteria. Indeed, in the sort of shadow-play that was the McMartin case, seven other local day care centers came under suspicion. The *Los Angeles Times* published one story after another about their closings after some McMartin enrollees alleged they were swapped for children there for the purposes of pornography and prostitution. The newspaper, in fact, featured eight separate stories about one center, the Peninsula Montessori, but never reported its reopening when police declined to file charges against the providers, until its owner complained to the editor.

Indictments

In this milieu of surmises, conjectures and rumors, the seven McMartin providers were indicted by a grand jury in March 1984 on 115 counts of child molestation and one count of conspiracy. A few weeks later an additional 208 counts were added, and they were promptly arrested. In a press conference, Assistant District Attorney Lael Rubin, newly appointed to the case, confidently announced that the preschool was a front for child pornography and that "enormous quantities of photographs" of the children were circulating through the dark and slimy underbelly of American society. Social worker MacFarlane agreed. In testimony before the U.S. House of Representatives, she described the McMartin Preschool as linked to an "organized operation of child predators, whose operation is designed to prevent detection, and is well insulated against legal intervention. . . [and that] may have greater financial, legal, and community resources than any of the agencies trying to uncover them." This touch of conspiracy thickened the plot, but the role of the devil as *agent provocateur* was not introduced until later that year.

Charges of Ritual Satanic Abuse

Enter Lawrence Pazder. Since the publication [in 1980] of *Michelle Remembers*, [a book about satanic ritual abuse, cowritten by Pazder] he had been traveling across North America, talking to mental health clinicians and law enforcement officers about satanic threats to children. Pazder's notion of ritual abuse, the term he had coined in 1981 to label the childhood memories of his erstwhile patient, Michelle, was going through a curiously accommodating transmutation. Michelle had never remembered sexual abuse by her satanic captors, thus Pazder's original definition of ritual abuse as "repeated physical, emotional, mental and spiritual assaults" that are carried out through the "systematic use of symbols, ceremonies, and machinations designed and orchestrated to attain malevolent effects," did not include it. Sensing the *Zeitgeist* [general mood of the times], perhaps, Pazder now tagged "sexual" to his list of ritually abusive assaults and told the timorous parents, social workers, law enforcement officers and district attorneys he met with that the McMartin Preschool case was at the center of an international satanic conspiracy. . . .

All the interrogators, including the parents, began asking the children different kinds of questions, sometimes using devil puppets as props, and comparing answers against checklists of satanic rituals, roles, ceremonies and holidays put together by New Christian Right crusaders. With the "ultimate evil" of ritual abuse as the rudder of their imagination, anything the children revealed was deemed plausible.

In the face of relentless grilling with this new demonic twist, the young children soon figured out that "round, unvarnish'd tales" were not what their interrogators wanted to hear. So they told other tales—"tales about the ritualistic ingestion of feces, urine, blood, semen and human flesh; the disinterment and mutilation of corpses; the sacrifices of infants; and the orgies with their day care providers costumed as devils and witches, in the classrooms, in tunnels under the center, and in car washes, airplanes, mansions, cemeteries, hotels, ranches, gourmet food stores, local gyms, churches, and hot air balloons." And they eventually named not only the seven McMartin providers as their ritual abusers, but their soccer coaches, babysitters, neighbors, and even their own parents, as well as local businesspeople, the mayor's wife, news reporters covering the story, television and film stars, and players on the Anaheim Angels baseball team. . . .

Preliminary Hearings

The rumors about devil worship were revealed during the preliminary hearing of the seven providers that began in June 1984 and lasted eighteen months—the longest hearing of its kind in the history of the United States. Thirteen children testified. In the face of blistering cross-examination by seven separate defense attorneys, some stood firm in their accounts of excursions to cemeteries where their providers hacked up dead bodies, to a house where a basement full of roaring lions terrified them, and to a church where black-robed strangers danced around the altar. Some wavered, though, and a few contradicted themselves completely after days on the witness stand.

In the end, the judge bound over all seven of the providers to stand trial on 135 counts of child molestation and conspiracy. Days later, newly elected District Attorney Ira Reiner dropped all of the charges against five of the providers, characterizing them as "incredibly weak." Peggy McMartin Buckey and her son Raymond were left to stand trial on 99 counts of molestation and one count of conspiracy.

A telephone survey revealed just how hot for certainty the community was about this case. Conducted by Duke University researchers, it found that 98 percent of the respondents believed Raymond Buckey was "definitely or probably guilty" of the charges against him, 93 percent believed the same about Peggy McMartin Buckey, 80 percent were sure the five other providers also were guilty, and 80 percent had no doubt that the providers had engaged in the acts of ritual abuse the children had described in the preliminary hearing. . . .

"Believe the Children"

"Believe the Children" was not just the mantra oft-repeated to invoke the social honor of the accusing children, but a political banner under which some of their parents came together to form the Believe the Children Organization, a clearinghouse for ritual abuse information and advocacy center. Through its efforts, the state of California passed legislation that allowed for closed-circuit television testimony of children in some criminal cases. Although it did not apply to legal proceedings already under way, including the McMartin Preschool case, the law heralded a wave of legislation that created special testimonial opportunities for children in the day care ritual abuse cases that kept cropping up as the moral panic triggered by the McMartin Preschool case spread across the country.

But by July 1987 it all came down to a question of final belief. The criminal trial of Peggy McMartin Buckey and her son Raymond on 100 counts of child molestation and conspiracy opened in a packed Los Angeles courtroom. . . .

The prosecution insisted that anything these fourteen children said about ritual abuse must be taken as truth; any discrepancy, contradiction or retraction must be seen as a consequence of their "accommodation" to the abuse and therefore as validation of the truth of their testimony. Because children cannot imagine what they have not experienced, the prosecution argued, their testimony requires no interpretation. The defense disagreed. It asserted that anything the children said about ritual abuse must be taken as what they believe to be the truth; any discrepancy, contradiction or retraction must be seen as an invalidation of the truth of their testimony. Because children can be naively led to believe they actually have experienced something they never have, the defense argued, their testimony requires careful interpretation. . . .

Seven months before the trial began, Judy Johnson was found dead in her home. The woman whose allegations started the case, whose psychiatric history including a recent period of hospitalization and a diagnosis of paranoid schizophrenia was withheld from the defense by the prosecution, drank herself to death over the Christmas holiday. The jury would never hear from the woman whose passions spun the plot of the ritual abuse narrative, nor from her then seven year old son whom the presiding had declared testimonially incompetent. . . .

A Moral Panic Runs Its Course

On November 2, 1989, the case of *People v. Buckey* went to the jury. Over the twenty-eight months of the trial 124 witnesses had testified, over 900 pieces of evidence had been introduced, 64,000 pages of transcript had accumulated, and 100 charges had been whittled down to 65 when parents had a change of mind and refused to let their children testify.

On January 18, 1990, the jury returned the verdicts. It acquitted Peggy McMartin Buckey of all of the charges against her, and Raymond Buckey of 29 of the 52 charges against him. The jury had deadlocked on the remaining 13 charges. In the hurry-to-get-it-over pace of an anticlimax, Buckey was retried on 8 of the strongest remaining charges. Once again the jury deadlocked and with the words "All right that's it," the judge dismissed all charges against Raymond Buckey. . . .

The McMartin Preschool case marks both the beginning and near-end of the day care ritual abuse moral panic. When it began, no one could get enough of it. The ritual abuse narrative "made sense" because it discursively linked the master symbols of that decade, personified the inchoate fears and anxieties of that time, and clarified moral positions. But by 1990, almost everyone had supped their fill of horror. The ritual abuse narrative had lost most of its Gothic appeal.

The beginning and the ending of a moral panic are always interesting, but it is what happened between the two—the scores of other day care ritual abuse cases the McMartin Preschool case triggered—that reveal the most about its volatility, perniciousness, and its extravagant irrationality.

The Recovered Memory Debate

Tiffany Danitz

In the 1990s a wave of adults made accusations of having been abused in childhood and then forgetting it for years until therapists helped them recover their memories. This was based on the idea of repressed-memory syndrome, in which abuses experienced in childhood are repressed, and seem to be completely forgotten, but cause psychological problems in adulthood. Supporters of the theory believe that the repressed memories should be recovered—brought back into consciousness and remembered—and confronted. Critics claim, however, that in many cases these memories are not "recovered" but rather completely false, the result of inappropriate use of hypnosis or other techniques by therapists. Investigations of therapists and lawsuits resulted. The following article reviews the repressed memory controversy and argues that it was a fad rather than a helpful way of understanding how childhood abuse affects people as adults.

Treatments ranging from frontal lobotomies to repressed-memory therapy for the neuroses or psychoses *du jour* are being touted in feature stories across the country, and Court TV is bubbling over with psychobabble. It is difficult to believe that just 100 years ago Americans pioneered the frontier without a therapist in tow.

Medical Diagnosis as Social Trend

"Much of psychiatric diagnoses and even a lot of medical diagnoses are a matter of fashion," says Greg Bloche, a health- and policy-law professor at Georgetown University and an ad-

Tiffany Danitz, "Making Up Memories? (Repressed Memory Syndrome)," *Insight on the News*, vol. 13, n. 46, December 15, 1997, pp. 14–15. Copyright © 1997 News World Communications, Inc. All rights reserved. Reproduced with permission of Insight on the News.

junct professor in public health at Johns Hopkins University. Early in [the twentieth] century, theorists expounded on the powers of electric shock to "cure" schizophrenia. And by the early forties some even supported the use of the prefrontal lobotomy as therapy, a fact to which the Kennedy family can attest: They believed lobotomy would calm the inchoate spirit of their daughter Rose-Marie [sister of former president John F. Kennedy] who suffered from mild retardation and a fabled Irish temper.

Fads generated through psychology and nineties self-indulgence often have resulted in diagnoses that lay in an "ambiguous realm" where empirical evidence may or may not support theories and opinions of the diagnostician, according to Bloche. He lists premenstrual syndrome; multiple personality disorder, or MPD; and the latest affliction, road rage (aggressive driving) as examples.

"When different forms of behavior or psychological phenomena capture people's attention, if it is an unwanted phenomenon, they give it a psychological label," he adds.

Repressed-Memory Syndrome

The latest pop-psychology fad to hit the newsstands and the courts was named "repressed-memory syndrome" therapy by Richard Ofshe, a forensic psychologist and author of *Making Monsters*. The therapy is rooted in Freudian psychoanalysis and a belief that the mind blocks distressing information, he says. Through the use of hypnosis, a therapist encourages a patient to experience a fantasy, like a nightmare, and then suggests to the patient that the experience really happened, according to Ofshe. This is said to release the repression and free the memory.

Laura Brown, a Seattle psychologist and member of the American Psychological Association, or APA, team that researched repressed memory, claims the very term is bogus. "There are various therapeutic approaches that look at or deal with traumatic amnesia," she says. "Most people have these re-calls not in therapy or as a result of therapy, but many times come to therapy because they have this recall."

Questionable Therapies Lead to Lawsuits

Tana Dineen, a psychologist and author of *Manufacturing Victims*, tells *Insight* that, if it becomes a matter of truth in advertising, "repressed memory is the first of the psychological products that will be pulled from the shelf," referring to a record settlement of $10.6 million awarded in November [1997] to an Illinois woman who sued her therapist for creating false memories of ritual sexual abuse. A few days earlier, during the last week of October, Texas filed criminal charges against four therapists in a similar lawsuit.

In the Illinois action, the day the court was to hear the civil case of *Burgus vs. Braun*, Patricia Burgus accepted a huge settlement offered by Bennett Braun and the hospital, Rush Presbyterian-St. Luke's Medical Center. Braun diagnosed Burgus with MPD after she began treatment for severe postpartum depression. During a six-year period, the hospital treated Burgus with medication, psychotherapy and hypnosis. She says she was persuaded to believe she had memories of being in a satanic cult, participating in ritual murder and sexually abusing her two children, ages 4 and 5, whom she was advised to admit to the hospital.

The Philadelphia-based False Memory Syndrome Foundation is an advocacy group for families affected by false-memory syndrome. It has researched 105 court cases involving repressed memory: One was dropped, 42 settled out of court, 53 are pending and nine went to trial.

Malpractice suits generally have consisted of civil-court battles where patients accuse their therapists of sexually assaulting them or using methods or techniques that violate the standard of care, says Bloche.

Memories of Past Abuse

Suzanne Hughes of Northern Virginia shares an experience similar to that of Burgus. Hughes, 31, says she was sexually abused as a child but never repressed the memory. At age 25, Hughes was suffering from postpartum depression when she lost her firstborn child to a congenital defect.

"When my oldest died it broke my heart," Hughes recalls. "I was crying all the time, I had mood swings and I started drinking." When she stopped imbibing, Hughes says she was haunted by constantly recurring memories of the sexual abuse she had suffered.

In 1990 Hughes admitted herself to a hospital, complaining of an eating disorder, depression and a history of being sexually abused. Her therapist diagnosed her with MPD composed of three alter personalities, but Hughes says she never believed the diagnosis.

Hughes contends that when she would resist the diagnosis she would be confined to the hospital for long stays and heavily medicated. "So I would give her a performance," she says. "If I got rid of this [in their eyes] I'd get my kid back." But if Hughes disagreed with the therapist, she says, she was told she wasn't participating in her therapy.

Trusting Only the Therapist

"She would put me on medicine and give me hypnotics to bring up my memories. She would have me draw pictures of my alters [alter egos] and my abuse," Hughes says. She alleges that her therapist gave her perfume, jewelry and renewed hope that her daughter would be returned to her whenever she would perform correctly. "The sicker I got, the more attention and rewards I got," says Hughes. She adds that everyone in her therapy group was required to read *The Courage to Heal*, a book that suggests that "if you think you have been sexually abused, then you have." This book was named in a

California lawsuit (*Mark vs. Zulli*) in which a woman falsely diagnosed with MPD and 400 alters was awarded $157,000 in a settlement.

Eventually Hughes was convinced that she and the other patients had been involved in a satanic cult in which they had been ritually sexually abused. Her therapist, she says, told the group, "See that mark? That is the mark they give you when you go through [a satanic] ritual." Hughes says she became afraid to go anywhere during a full moon. She was alienated from family and friends and told to trust only her therapist. When she would panic, the therapist would get her into a safe house, "making me believe the cult was coming after me." But most devastating to Hughes was being told that her daughter had been fathered by one of the satanists in the cult and then ritually murdered.

A New Diagnosis

In the winter of 1993, Hughes' therapist became ill and Hughes had to find a new one. Jean Marie Amiri treated her as a sexual-abuse survivor and did not diagnose her with MPD. Within six months, Hughes was recovering. The new therapist neither used hypnosis nor hospitalized her, says Hughes. After all, "I was just a sick, depressed mother who missed her 18-month-old baby when she died," she said.

Does such an experience sound far-fetched? Then consider this landmark criminal case in Texas in which four therapists and an administrator were charged with defrauding insurance companies of millions of dollars using repressed-memory therapy. The defendants targeted people with "large and un-limited" lifetime insurance policies for inpatient treatment. They diagnosed the patients with MPD. Then they used suggestive questioning while the patients were drugged or under hypnosis, isolated them from the outside world and held group discussions encouraging "stories" of alleged abuse. The patients were led to believe that they were members of a satanic cult and had abused their own family members, some of whom then were admitted for treatment, all according to the grand-jury indictment.

Patients Made Sicker

Ofshe argues that every case of repressed-memory therapy that he has examined shows that patients decline, and the cases often involve tales of sexual abuse and the occult. "There is no point in doing this unless you come up with something really ugly. If it is not bad enough that your dad sexually abused you, then your mother was there. And if that isn't bad enough, then it was satanic and the cult made you pregnant and you had to eat the baby. Because the patient is stressed and upset from this, they get them in the hospital and drug the hell out of them, which will make matters worse."

Brown counters that the memories of satanic abuse really are more about pornography and child prostitution—problems that do exist. While some cite cases such as these as examples of science gone awry, Brown says the only crime these therapists committed was to believe their patients.

Bloche agrees that the Texas case should be taken in stride. He says, "It is a dangerous business for courts to be convicting people of crimes for testimony based on repressed memory. It is another thing entirely to say that the person who administered that treatment is committing a crime just because the treatment is not empirically proven."

A Lifegiving Culture

It may even be that the lawsuits in these cases themselves are part of the pop culture, reflecting growing litigiousness threatening proponents of all types of therapeutic practice. "I find it a very frightening trend," says Brown, "because the people being sued gave what they believed to be a real diagnosis and to my understanding treated it in a way they thought it should be treated. It is bad for the courts to be deciding they don't like a given diagnosis."

The APA has been split over repressed memory. And Ofshe contends that this is only an example of the field of psychology weeding out quackery as the medical profession did in earlier stages. He says, "Myths don't collapse of their own weight. They collapse because something forces them in two directions."

Sexual Abuse in
the Catholic Church

Michael Rezendes

In 2002 a team of reporters at the Boston Globe *revealed that
for many decades, Catholic priests had been sexually abusing
children, that the Catholic Church hierarchy had actively covered
up the scandal, and, that, in doing so, the church had exposed
further children to abuse. Michael Rezendes is a member of the*
Boston Globe *Spotlight Team that won the 2003 Pulitzer Prize
for Public Service for reporting on the sexual abuse in the Catholic Church. In the following piece, Rezendes recounts how, after
the reporters uncovered the scandal, more than 450 priests in the
United States were forced to resign due to charges of sexual misconduct. He also describes the reactions of the American public
and the Catholic Church to these charges. Cardinal Bernard F.
Law, who resigned as archbishop of Boston in December 2002,
currently serves as the archpriest of the Basilica di Santa Maria
Maggior in Rome. Cardinal Joseph Ratzinger, who oversaw the
church tribunal hearings on clergy sexual abuse in 2002, is now
Pope Benedict XlV.*

On December 13, 2002, Cardinal Bernard F. Law resigned
as archbishop of Boston, his embattled leadership in
America's most Catholic major city no longer viable. "To all
those who have suffered from my shortcomings and mistakes.
I both apologize and from them beg forgiveness," he said.

Law's public act of contrition was a dramatic departure
from the imperious pose he often struck as the nation's senior
prelate and its most influential Catholic. And he stepped down
only after a yearlong exposé of clergy sexual abuse by a team

of reporters at the *Boston Globe*. That journalistic endeavor differed markedly from previous efforts by the *Globe* and other newspapers to report on abuse in the Catholic Church. In the summer of 2001, the *Globe's* Spotlight Team was asked to investigate Law's role in the reassignment of a notorious pedophile, the Rev. John J. Geoghan. But after learning that Geoghan might be only the most obvious sign of a larger problem, the team of reporters also set out to measure the full extent of clerical abuse in the Archdiocese of Boston, and the response of Law and his bishops.

The Clergy Sex Abuse Scandal

By the time Law resigned, the *Globe* had published more than 800 stories. Characterized by escalating revelations of sexual misconduct, the stories cited thousands of pages of the Church's own records to reveal institutional forgiveness of abusive priests, consistent indifference to victims, and compelling evidence of a decades-long cover-up by a succession of cardinals and their bishops. Today, the number of priests accused of sexual misconduct in the Boston archdiocese during the last four decades exceeds 150. Twenty-four priests have been suspended from active ministry. More than 500 people have filed clergy-abuse claims. And donations to the Church have dropped by about half, leaving the archdiocese in fiscal free-fall.

The implosion has reverberated far beyond Boston. News organizations across the country and throughout the world have used the *Globe's* reporting as a template and have launched investigations of their own. Since January of 2002, when the *Globe* published its first stories on the cover-up in Boston, more than 450 priests in the United States have been forced from their jobs because of sexual misconduct allegations. And four bishops, including Law, have resigned after being accused of abuse, admitting to sexual misconduct, or acknowledging they failed to remove known child molesters from active ministry. . . .

But the complete story of clerical abuse in the Catholic Church has yet to be told. And in the absence of further reporting, and desperately needed clinical studies, the Church and its critics will continue to debate whether the number of accused priests points to a crisis in the Catholic Church and its celibate clergy, or merely reflects the prevalence of child sexual abuse in the American population.

Thousands of Victims

Nevertheless, it's clear that the number of accused priests revealed thus far is only a fraction of the whole, and that the true extent of clergy abuse in the Catholic Church remains unknown. Complete Church records on allegations of clergy sexual misconduct have been aired in only a few of the 195 dioceses in the United States. And even in those instances, the number of accused is nothing more than a measure of those whose victims had the courage to step forward and identify their abusers. It also appears that Church officials at the highest levels have underestimated the problem. In November 2002, Cardinal Joseph Ratzinger, the Vatican official now in charge of overseeing the new Church tribunals hearing cases of clergy abuse, said that "less than one percent" of priests had sexually molested children. But a survey by the *New York Times* found that, in the few American dioceses where Church officials have released the names of all accused priests, or where judges and prosecutors have forced the Church to air the information, the estimates range from 5.3 percent in the Boston archdiocese to 6.2 percent in Baltimore and 7.7 percent in Manchester, New Hampshire. And that survey, completed at the end of 2002, undercounted the total number of accused priests that have come to light in the Boston archdiocese, meaning that the percentage of abusive clerics in Boston is higher than 5.3 percent. . . .

And yet, both the Church and its critics have said the unprecedented scandal erupting in the wake of the *Globe*'s reporting has had one overarching benefit: Thousands of victims who suffered in silence and now call themselves survivors have been freed from the secrecy and shame of sexual abuse and are able to live more fulfilling lives. At the same time, it seems reasonable to believe, or at least hope, that countless children entering the Church under new child protection policies are being spared the debilitating abuse that too often characterized the past.

The *Globe*'s investigation was triggered by a routine court filing by Cardinal Law in June of 2001. That document—Law's response to the allegations in 84 lawsuits filed by victims of John Geoghan—contained a brief yet startling admission: in 1984, Law had assigned Geoghan to a suburban parish knowing that Geoghan had been accused of molesting seven boys in the same extended family. Law, writing in the archdiocesan newspaper, *The Pilot*, later explained that the church, like the larger society, knew little of the intractable nature of child sexual abuse when he assigned Geoghan to St. Julia's parish in Weston, where Geoghan went on to molest more children. And Law's attorney, Wilson D. Rogers Jr., writing in the same edition, assured parishioners that each of Geoghan's assignments following the first complaint of abuse had been approved by Geoghan's physicians.

Researching Allegations of Abuse

The *Globe* Spotlight Team—editor Walter V. Robinson and reporters Matt Carroll, Sacha Pfeiffer, and myself, Michael Rezendes—began to test those assertions. In particular, we wanted to know how Law had been informed of Geoghan's molestations, who had informed him, and exactly how much he knew about Geoghan's pedophilia when he gave the predator priest another church assignment and continuing access to children.

Working under the direction of special projects editor Ben Bradlee Jr., we found, within a matter of days, that Geoghan was only one of a large number of priests who had sexually molested children and been given new assignments. In fact, we were told, Church officials had been quietly settling claims against sexually abusive priests for at least a decade, often with "hush money" and terms that prevented the victims from ever speaking about the abuse or the settlements. It was an efficient arrangement that seemed to serve the interests of all involved: Victims received financial compensation, although often quite modest, and were spared public embarrassment. Their lawyers received one-third or more of the settlements, for minimal labor. And the Church avoided scandal.

But proving that the transactions had taken place was another matter. The Church, unlike government agencies or publicly traded corporations, operates with virtually no public disclosure requirements. The Constitutional guarantee of freedom of religion gives Church officials significant insulation from civil oversight. And in Catholic Boston, decades of deference to Church officials had discouraged criminal prosecutors from prying into Church affairs. And when it came to the Geoghan case, 10,000 pages of Church records that had accumulated in the course of the 84 lawsuits against Law and other Church officials had been sealed by a highly unusual confidentiality order issued by the state's Superior Court.

Martin Baron, the *Globe*'s newly named editor, decided to challenge that order. . . .

Confronting the Church

On September 6, 2001, more than a half-dozen lawyers were calling on the power of a judge as they made their arguments on the *Globe*'s motion to lift the confidentiality order in the Geoghan case. Attorneys for the archdiocese, standing before Superior Court Judge Constance M. Sweeney, made several points. Citing the Constitution's guarantee of freedom of religion, they asserted a right to keep church records private. They also argued that the *Globe* had no standing in the case and said that lifting the order would imperil the ability of Church officials to receive a fair trial. Representing the *Globe*, attorney Jonathan M. Albano noted that the public is routinely granted access to evidentiary files in civil lawsuits, and argued that the public's overall interest in child sexual abuse should prevail over the privacy concerns of Church. Attorneys for the victims backed Albano.

Judge Sweeney, the product of 16 years of Catholic education, peppered all sides with questions. At one point she asked Church lawyers for a more complete rationale for setting aside the customary rules of evidence in keeping Church records in the Geoghan case from the public. But she also told the *Globe's* lawyer that her "bottom line" would be a fair trial for Law and his assistants—offering not a clue about what her final ruling might be.

The next day, September 7, the Spotlight Team learned the names of more than 30 priests who had been accused of sexual misconduct. While awaiting Sweeney's decision, the four reporters established a two-track reporting process. One was an attempt to pierce the secrecy surrounding the out-of-court settlements involving accused clergy, while trying to measure the extent of abuse in the archdiocese and the response of the Church leaders. The other was an effort to learn everything possible about Geoghan's career, the scores of victims he had left behind during three decades as a priest, and most important, the evident failure of Church officials to stop him. . . .

How the Church Handled the Allegations

While working on the data base, we also fanned out to interview priests and victims of clergy abuse to learn more about how the Church dealt with allegations of sexual misconduct by its clerics. What we learned was often devastating: The Rev. Ronald R. Paquin was at the wheel during a car accident—

possibly involving alcohol—in which a Haverhill teenager entrusted to his care was killed. The Rev. Paul R. Shanley, a celebrated street priest during the 1970s, seduced sexually troubled teenagers during counseling sessions. And the Rev. Paul J. Mahan, a popular priest in a working class section of Boston, molested young boys during boating trips off Boston's affluent North Shore.

When we compared notes, a disturbing pattern emerged: Many of the victims were from large, lower-income families with absent fathers and overburdened mothers grateful for the help and attention of a Catholic priest. Patrick McSorley, for instance, described how Geoghan molested him after dropping by his apartment in a public housing project to offer condolences following his father's suicide. Predator priests, by zeroing in on lower-income, fatherless boys, were sexually exploiting children most in need of fatherly attention. They were also targeting families most likely to remain silent—and least likely to be believed if they talked.

In late November of 2001, nearly four months after the Spotlight Team began its investigation, Judge Sweeney ruled in favor of the *Globe*'s motion to lift the confidentiality order in the Geoghan case, saying that the public's interest in child sexual abuse outweighed the privacy claims of the archdiocese.

Church Knowledge of Abuses

The Church appealed. But by that time Sweeney had also directed attorneys in the Geoghan case to re-submit the records that were missing from the public file. Those records contained startling revelations about Church knowledge of Geoghan's abuses. They included excerpts of a deposition taken from Joanne Mueller, a single mother who said she complained to Church officials after a horrific evening in the early 1970s, before Law arrived in Boston, when her four sons, aged 5 to 12, tearfully confessed that Geoghan had been mo-

lesting them. It was just one of at least six documented instances where adults—in one instance a fellow priest—had
complained about Geoghan's molestations, all to no avail. The
re-filed records also included a 1984 letter to Law from one of
his top deputies, Bishop John M. D'Arcy, protesting Geoghan's
assignment at St. Julia's because of the priest's "history of ho-
mosexual involvement with young boys." Geoghan had not
slipped through the cracks, as Law implied in his column in
The Pilot. To the contrary, his assignment had been contested
at the highest levels of the archdiocese after decades of complaints.

With these records in hand, the *Globe* received another
Church document, one of more recent vintage and addressed
to the newspaper's lawyer. "It has been brought to my attention that certain reporters of your client, the *Boston Globe*,
have been making inquiry of a number of priests of the Archdiocese of Boston," wrote Wilson D. Rogers Jr., the lead attorney for the archdiocese. Rogers claimed that the interviews
were based on information we had obtained from the confidential Geoghan files. "In the event that the *Boston Globe* in
any way further disseminates these materials, either by way of
inquiry or publication," Rogers continued, "I will seek appropriate sanctions against both your client and Bingham Dana
[the paper's law firm]."

In fact, Mitchell Garabedian, the attorney for Geoghan's
victims, had excerpted portions of the confidential files and
inserted them into the public record as exhibits attached to
various legal motions. It was a tactic that, in effect, made portions of the confidential documents public. In any case, the
Globe ignored Rogers's letter and, in late December, the Appeals Court upheld Judge Sweeney's decision to lift the confidentiality order. Rogers never followed up on his threat.

The court gave attorneys in the case 30 days to publicly
file the 10,000 pages of previously sealed documents. In the
meantime, we quickly prepared a two-part series about

Geoghan. Part one would be built on a foundation of records we had culled from the public files; part two on some of Geoghan's psychiatric records, which would be delivered to the plaintiffs after the Appeals Court ruling but before the release of the 10,000 pages of previously filed documents. Weeks before publication, we also requested interviews with the Cardinal and other Church officials, even offering to submit questions in writing. But, with only two days remaining before publication, Law's spokeswoman said the archdiocese would not even consider our questions.

The Bishop Apologizes

The Geoghan series was published on January 6 and January 7, 2002, and the effect was like setting a match to gasoline. Two days later, on January 9, Law held an extraordinary news conference where he issued the first of several apologies, fielded questions from reporters, and assured parishioners that no priest accused of sexually abusing a minor remained in active ministry. . . .

On January 31, we published the results of our five-month investigation of clerical abuse in the archdiocese. It was another bombshell. Over the previous 10 years, the church had secretly settled sexual abuse allegations against 70 of its priests. The story undermined what remained of Law's credibility: Geoghan was no aberration, only a symtptom of a much larger problem.

Yet the Cardinal's credibility was eroded still further on a Saturday in early February 2002, when he abruptly removed two pastors—one a regional vicar with oversight of 19 parishes—after reviewing evidence in the Church's own files showing that they were accused of sexually molesting in the past. Five days later, Law removed six more in a process that would continue, leading to the suspension of a total of 24 clerygmen over a 12-month period.

Our reporting might have trailed off there. But the Spotlight Team stories were accompanied by the *Globe* telephone numbers and e-mail addresses of the reporters, and an invitation to contact the paper with more information about abusive priests. Scores of victims responded, frequently with tales of abuse they had never before revealed, not even to spouses or other family members. In the meantime, the state attorney general and five district attorneys launched criminal investigations that would lead to charges against a half-dozen priests. But the vast majority of allegations against Catholic clergy fell outside the criminal statute of limitations. So it was the victims stepping forward to tell their stories, and the lawsuits many of them would file, that drove our stories through the remainder of 2002.

CHAPTER 4

Perspectives on the Treatment and Prevention of Child Abuse

Chapter Preface

In the years since the passage of the Child Abuse Prevention and Treatment Act (CAPTA) of 1974, a large and complicated system has developed in the United States to try and deal with the problem of child abuse. Child Protective Service (CPS) agencies in the states work to investigate allegations of abuse and neglect. When the allegations are found to be true, they take action to end the abuse through methods ranging from family counseling to removing the children and placing them in foster care. Approximately five hundred thousand children were in foster care across the country in 2007.

No one disputes that CPS agencies—and their private partners—are an improvement over the days when no one worked to protect children from abuse. The current system does have many critics, however, who feel that in too many cases it fails to do the best job possible of helping at-risk children.

The sad story of Rilya Wilson, which made national headlines in 2002, exemplifies many of the criticisms that have been directed at the CPS system. In this case, the Florida state CPS agency—the Department of Children and Families (DCF)—admitted in 2002 that it had completely lost track of five-year-old Rilya. Rilya was placed in foster care by the state in 2000, but her caseworker failed to visit the child as required. Instead, the caseworker filed false reports claiming she had checked on Rilya and the girl was fine. By the time this situation was discovered, no one from the CPS agency had seen Rilya in years. One of her foster caregivers, Geralyn Graham, said that she had given the child to CPS workers in early 2001 and had not seen her since. It eventually came to light that Graham had a history of mental health problems and criminal behavior that should have disqualified her from becoming a foster caregiver, something the DCF had failed to discover. While in jail on fraud charges, Graham allegedly admitted to murdering Rilya Wilson, and was charged with that crime in 2004. As of July 2007, no one had been able to find Rilya Wilson or her remains.

There is no question that Florida's child protection system failed Rilya Wilson. A expert panel convened by Florida governor Jeb Bush in 2002 found that both Rilya's caseworker and that caseworker's supervisor had been incompetent, and that the DCF in general had many shortcomings. It went on to note, however, that this was not surprising as the DCF suffered from inadequate funding, staffing, and attention. In doing so, the panel echoed complaints about CPS agencies across the nation.

The Rilya Wilson case and what it represents is just one of the many challenges facing the effort to prevent abuse and improve the well-being of children in the United States. This chapter presents examples of existing efforts to help children, their critics, and suggestions as to what should be done differently.

The Government Must Invest in Prevention

Thomas L. Birch

In the following selection, which was originally presented in 2004 as testimony before the House Committee on Ways and Means, Thomas L. Birch argues that what the government spends on child abuse prevention and child protection falls far short of what government agencies estimate is needed. He states that treating the problems created by child abuse is not as effective as preventing child abuse in the first place. Rather than spend money addressing the problems of juvenile delinquency and adult criminality, mental illness, substance abuse, and chronic health problems that are the consequences of child abuse, he argues, it would be better to prevent abuse through community-based, in-home services to at-risk families. A range of services, such as voluntary home visits, family support services, parenting education, and respite care, Birch suggests, can work together to create a community plan to prevent child abuse and neglect.

Thomas L. Birch is the legislative counsel for the National Child Abuse Coalition, which consists of twenty-five national organizations working together to focus attention on the protection of children and the prevention of child maltreatment.

When we look at federal, state and local government spending on child welfare services, we see that we are investing in an outcome that no one wants—the placement of children in foster care. We are spending well over $16 billion each year to subsidize the foster care and adoptive placements of children who have been so seriously abused and neglected,

Thomas L. Birch, "Statement of Thomas L. Birch, Legislative Counsel, National Child Abuse Coalition," *To Review Federal and State Oversight of Child Welfare Programs: Hearing Before the Subcommittee on Human Resources of the Committee on Ways and Means, U.S. House of Representatives, One Hundred Eighth Congress, Second Session, January 28, 2004.* Washington, D.C: U.S. G.P.O., 2004, pp. 98–102.

so injured and in such danger that they are no longer safe to be left at home with their parents. A fraction of that amount is spent on prevention and intervention services to protect children from such severe harm.

No one would argue that we should not be paying to protect the children who have been the most seriously injured. But the fact is that the United States spends billions of dollars on programs that deal with the results of our failure to invest real money to prevent and treat child abuse and neglect.

Because our system is weighted toward protecting the most seriously injured children, we wait until it gets so bad that we have to step in. Far less attention in policy or funding is directed at preventing harm to children from ever happening in the first place or providing the appropriate services and treatment needed by families and children victimized by abuse or neglect.

In 2004, looking at the federal child welfare budget for Title IV-F [section of the Social Security Act that provides federal reimbursement to states for the costs of placing children in foster homes], the federal government pays out over $7 billion for out-of-home placements. Contrast that with funds [from several acts that] together add up to less than $900 million for prevention and intervention services to children and their families. For every federal dollar spent on foster care and adoption subsidies, we spend less than thirteen cents in federal child welfare funding on preventing and treating child abuse and neglect.

It is not enough for the federal government to provide services only for foster care and adoption; we have to put together additional resources to help states and communities build their capacity to support preventive services and treatment services as well. But until we reorder our overall budget priorities and begin allocating significant resources to prevention, we will never stop the flow of children onto our nation's foster care rolls. Putting dollars aside for prevention is sound investing, not luxury spending.

The Spending Gap

When we look at what we should be spending to improve the child protective service system and support community-based programs for preventing child abuse and neglect, we discover an enormous spending gap in prevention and protection.

We have a spending gap in this country of almost $13 billion in services to prevent child abuse and to intervene on behalf of children known to the child protection system. In 2000, spending in federal, state and local dollars for child protective services and preventive services amounts to only about $2.9 billion of the estimated $15.9 billion total cost of what ought to be spent on those services.

According to the Urban Institute, states reported spending $20 billion on child welfare in 2000, and they could categorize how $15.7 billion of the funds were used. Of that amount, $9.1 billion was spent for out-of-home placements, $1.8 billion on administration, $1.9 billion on adoption, and $2.9 billion (about 18 percent) on all other services, including prevention, family preservation and support services, and child protective services. . . .

The Costs of Abuse

First, consider the cost to child protective services of 1) investigating the reports of child abuse and neglect that were accepted in 2000 and 2) providing some basic services to the victims of child maltreatment in that year. When we look at the expense of investigating the 1.726 million children who were screened in for further assessment, plus the expense of providing services to the 879,000 substantiated child victims and to the 385,000 children in unsubstantiated reports who also received some services, we come up with a total cost of $5.9 billion.

We should not, here, overlook the unacceptable fact that nearly half the victims of child maltreatment in fact receive no services at all. One of the great tragedies of our system for protecting children is the hundreds of thousands of children—over 392,000 (45%) victims of child abuse in 2000—who received no services whatsoever: suspected abuse reported, report investigated, report substantiated, case closed. . . .

The CPS [Child Protective Services] spending shortfall amounts to a failure to invest in a system that could successfully protect children from abuse and neglect. When examining the actual dollars spent, the gap in CPS funding—a spending shortfall of nearly $3 billion—must be held accountable for many of the barriers to the adequate protection of children. Failing to invest in a working child protection system results in a national failure to keep children free from harm.

The Failure to Invest in Prevention

Second, consider the cost of preventive services—$10 billion if offered to the three million child maltreatment victims identified in the HHS [U.S. Department of Health and Human Services] National Incidence Study III—and I am not even talking about cost of offering voluntary, universal preventive services to families. That's a total cost of $15.9 billion. Yet, in 2000, states spent only $2.9 billion in federal, state and local funds on protective and preventive services for children. Our national child welfare policy represents a morally unacceptable failure to invest in this system.

These are conservative cost figures. When adjusted to account for inflation, data indicate that investigations by child protective service agencies cost approximately $990 per case. The cost per case to provide basic in-home services such as homemaker assistance or family counseling is $3,295. These costs are low to start with. Pay scales in child welfare are generally low and noncompetitive—significantly lower, for example, than salaries for teachers, school counselors, nurses and public-health social workers—which brings these costs in at an unrealistically low level.

What does the spending gap mean in terms of the child welfare workforce? Ninety percent of states report having difficulty in recruiting and retaining child welfare workers, because of issues like low salaries, high caseloads, insufficient training and limited supervision, and the turnover of child welfare workers—estimated to be between 30 and 40 percent annually nationwide. When we look at caseloads for child welfare workers, the average is double the recommended caseload, and obviously much higher in many jurisdictions.

Prevention Reduces Crime, School Failure

Our present system of treating abused and neglected children and offering some help to troubled families is overworked and inadequate to the task. We need to reorganize the current child protection system to come within the framework of a broader family support system. Hundreds of thousands of children are currently identified as having been abused, but receive no services to prevent further abuse. We must focus attention on children and families known to the system in order to prevent reoccurrence of abuse, as well as provide services to families earlier, before problems become severe.

For more than twenty years, the federal government's attention has concentrated on a restricted approach to child abuse and neglect, in many ways preventing the development of a major federal attack on the problem. As a result, the prevention of maltreatment of children, which lies at the root of many of this nation's social ills, has been marginalized.

We know that child abuse prevention fights crime, because research has shown us time after time that victims of child abuse are more likely to engage in criminality later in life, that childhood abuse increases the odds of future delinquency and adult criminality overall by 40 percent.

We know that preventing child maltreatment helps to prevent failure in school. Typically abused and neglected children suffer poor prospects for success in school, exhibiting poor initiative, language and other developmental delays, and a disproportionate amount of incompetence and failure. Ensuring that children are ready to learn means ensuring that children are safe at home with the kind of nurturing care that all children deserve.

We know that preventing child abuse can help to prevent disabling conditions in children. Physical abuse of children can result in brain damage, mental retardation, cerebral palsy, and learning disorders.

Prevention Reduces Social Cost of Physical and Mental Illness

Groundbreaking research conducted by the Centers for Disease Control [CDC] in collaboration with Kaiser Permanente shows us that childhood abuse is linked with behaviors later in life which result in the development of chronic diseases that cause death and disability, such as heart disease, cancer, chronic lung and liver diseases, and skeletal fracture. Similarly, the CDC research shows that adult victims of child maltreatment are more likely to engage in early first intercourse, have an unintended pregnancy, have high lifetime numbers of sexual partners, and suffer from depression and suicide attempts.

We know that women who suffered serious assaults in childhood experience more episodes of depression, posttraumatic stress, and substance abuse, demonstrating a relationship between childhood trauma and adult psychopathology, as well as links between childhood neglect and later alcohol problems in women.

Finally, looking at the consequences of child maltreatment, we find that among homeless people, many of them, especially homeless women, reported serious family problems or a history of sexual or physical abuse as children that predisposed them to homelessness as adults.

An analysis of the costs of child abuse and neglect in the United States looking at the direct costs of hospitalizations, chronic health problems, mental health care, child welfare services, law enforcement intervention, and the judicial process totals over $24 billion annually. When we add the indirect costs from special education, additional health and mental health care, juvenile delinquency and adult criminality, as well as lost productivity, the total annual cost of child abuse and neglect in the United States amounts to more than $94 billion. We cannot sustain this drain of human and financial capital when we know how to support families and prevent abuse from occurring in the first place.

Investing in Prevention Is Cost Effective

Preventing child abuse is cost effective. Over ten years ago (1992) a report by the General Accounting Office looking at evaluations of child abuse prevention efforts found that "total federal costs of providing prevention programs for low-income populations were nearly offset after four years."

Community-based, in-home services to overburdened families are far less costly than the damage inflicted on children that leads to outlays for child protective services, law enforcement, courts, foster care, health care and the treatment of adults recovering from child abuse. A range of services, such as voluntary home-visiting, family support services, parent mutual support programs, parenting education, and respite care contribute to a community's successful strategy to prevent child abuse and neglect. To be eligible for federal child welfare assistance, states should be required to develop a prevention plan including effective programs identified to carry out the prevention work of community-based programs serving families and children. . . .

It is our collective responsibility and our duty to America's children and the nation's future to work toward that goal.

The Government Should Invest in Family Preservation

The Economist

Over five hundred thousand children are in foster care in the United States. According to the 2004 Pew Commission on Children in Foster Care, the reason why so many children are in foster care for so long is because of how the federal government funds the foster care system. In the following article, the Economist *magazine argues that programs that focus on family preservation, while expensive, cost no more than the current system but would provide long-term savings in terms of producing better-educated children, less delinquency, and more united, less abusive families. The* Economist *suggests that flexible use of federal money is necessary to provide the help that families and children in trouble need.*

Children are being taken into care too quickly and for too long.

The budget bill passed recently by the House of Representatives includes around $50 billion in spending cuts, many of them aimed at federal programmes for the poor. This includes trims of around $5 billion in child support, $600m for children in foster care and around $700m in food stamps. A similar bill from the Senate contains $34 billion of cuts with far fewer swipes at social-welfare programmes, but both bills include between $60 billion and $70 billion in tax cuts that disproportionately favour the rich. Child advocates are enraged. As states consider reforming their child-welfare systems, big cuts in social services are not helpful.

Tales of missing, starved, abused and even murdered children in adopted homes and foster shelters are alarmingly common. Some escape the attention of over-burdened social workers; others are shuttled from one foster-care placement to another for years on end. Last year, a Pew Commission on Children in Foster Care concluded that, because of the way federal funding works, children were plucked from their families too soon and left to fester in the system for too long. And although judges play a critical role in moving children to safety, family courts are among the most under-funded in the system, with few incentives to attract top lawyers and judges and little collaboration between the courts and child-welfare agencies. Dependency lawyers tend to be overworked and underpaid, with predictably bad results for the children they represent.

500,000 Children in Foster Care

More than 500,000 children are in foster care in America, most of them black or Latino. They remain in the system for an average of three years. These children, typically placed in the state's care after suffering abuse and neglect at home, often endure a demoralising parade of indifferent caseworkers, lawyers, judges, teachers and foster parents, who offer little real support in their quest for a stable home. For those who cannot return to their birth parents, the situation is grim: in 2003, 119,000 children in America were waiting to be adopted, 67% of whom had been in foster care for more than two years, according to the Department of Health and Human Services (HHS).

When such children "age out", or turn 18, as 18,000–20,000 do every year, they are suddenly cut off from all special services such as housing and counselling. Studies show that they disproportionately drop out of college, become homeless and unemployed, turn to drugs and alcohol and spend time in jail.

The federal government pays around half America's $22 billion child-welfare bill, according to the Urban Institute; the rest comes from state and local governments. But states have not been held accountable for how they spend this money. In an extensive three-year audit of state child-welfare systems, the HHS found that not a single state was in compliance with federal safety standards. When it came to the seven federal standards used to assess children's programmes, some of which are almost embarrassingly basic (e.g. "Children are first and foremost protected from abuse and neglect" and "Children receive adequate services to meet their physical and mental health needs"), 16 states did not meet any of them, and no state met more than two. The federal agency is now running a second round of audits, to assess whether states are now complying with their own improvement plans.

"We are spending a great deal of money to damage children," says Marcia Robinson Lowry, director of Children's Rights, an advocacy group. There are no real consequences for states when they fail to meet federal targets, she argues, so class-action lawsuits are the only recourse. Children's Rights has represented foster children in 13 court cases in the past decade. Most of these have ended in a court-ordered settlement that sets the group as a watchdog over a state's mismanaged and overburdened social-services department.

The Need for Flexible Services

But using the courts to solve America's child-welfare problems is expensive and inefficient. The best answer, many think, is for states to spend money on keeping families together, by investing in services such as child care and counselling, rather than putting children in care. This would require allowing states to use federal funding in different ways. Most federal dollars now begin flowing to states only when children are removed from their families, giving states a perverse incentive to keep children in foster care, explains Carol Emig, the director of the Pew Commission. Instead, the commission suggests that states need a little more federal money to cover all children, not just poor ones, and the flexibility to create a range of services that might keep children from entering care or help them leave care safely.

Such a change carries quite a price-tag: $5 billion over ten years. But advocates say it will bring long-term savings by producing better educated, less delinquent children and more united families. If states safely reduce their foster-care rolls, they can then reinvest dollars earmarked for foster care in other child-welfare services. Meanwhile, federal reviews will hold states to their programme promises. President George Bush has proposed, alternatively, that states should convert their foster-care entitlement programmes into block grants. That would give flexibility at first but, over time, it would amount to a cut in funds.

States and cities can already apply for waivers from federal funding restraints; some 20 states have waivers now. Advocates of flexible funding point to Illinois, a waiver recipient, where the foster-care population has been cut in half and adoptions have more than doubled since 1997. And in late October [2005] officials in New York City announced that the number of children in foster care has dropped to around 18,000, half of what it was six years ago. Once home to one of the worst foster-care systems in the country, the city now works to keep families intact and help them look after their children rather than taking the youngsters away. As a result, "the spigot coming into the system has been narrowed", explains David Tobis, director of the Child Welfare Fund, a local organisation. The money saved from federal entitlements—an estimated $27m in the fiscal year that began in July—will be put back into preventive services.

October also saw Arnold Schwarzenegger, California's governor, sign into law a number of bills to help the state's foster children—more than 80,000 of them. Most of the new laws will help teenagers when they turn 18, by making sure they stay in college and have somewhere to live.

Amid all the horror stories, it can be easy to lose sight of the people who make foster care work. After describing the madness of waiting all day at court to represent a client, only to receive five minutes of a distracted judge's time, one social worker goes on to describe some of the good foster parents she has met. Her voice grows tender when she describes one couple who have taken in a young, physically disabled child. "You tend to hear about the system's flaws", she explains. "But there are also so many other amazing things."

The Foster Care System Must Do Better

Lenny Levinson

The following article is a first-person account from a case manager in the New York City foster care system. Lenny Levinson describes the system as disorganized and overwhelmed. He argues that there are so many children in the system and so few caseworkers and so much unproductive bureaucracy that despite working hard and genuinely caring about children and their families, the caseworkers at the New York City Administration for Children's Services are prevented from doing their jobs effectively. This is because the administration is not well designed, he argues; as a result, there is enormous waste of available money, human resources, and, ultimately, the future lives of the foster children the agencies fail to protect. He argues that in order to serve children better, the foster care system must provide each child with a consistent caseworker, supervisor, and manager, who works directly with him or her each week, and must eliminate the layers of bureaucracy and lessen the paperwork so that caseworkers can spend the bulk of their time working directly with children and their families and foster families.

As I write these words, I am crammed along with approximately 70 other individuals into an overheated waiting room on the fifth floor of Brooklyn Family Court. I am experiencing anxiety, because every sizable New York City public gathering contains at least one raving lunatic. The one in this group is seated on a bench about 10 yards away. She is a well-dressed, heavyset, thirtyish black woman who is loudly denouncing the Hispanic male caseworker from the New York City Administration for Children's Services (ACS), who is sit-

Lenny Levinson, "Inside New York's Foster Care System: 34,000 Kids Trying to Catch a Break," *The Village Voice*, vol. 45, no. 24, June 2000, pp. 40–47. Copyright © 2000 Village Voice Media, Inc. Reproduced with the permission of *The Village Voice*.

ting in the far corner, calmly reading the *Daily News*. According to the woman's tirade, the caseworker snatched away her children, alleging she was too mentally disturbed to care for them.

Is the mother merely angry, perhaps justifiably, or on the verge of violence? And what in the name of heaven or hell am I doing in this potentially hazardous situation? I am not a journalist or anthropologist, but an ACS caseworker from the Office of Contract Agency Case Management (OCACM). I am scheduled to attend a hearing concerning a child on my caseload whom I have never seen. . . .

A Day at Court

I calm myself by contemplating my upcoming court appearance. I must testify on behalf of a four-year-old boy who recently was returned to foster care following an unsupervised weekend home visit with his putative birth father. The child allegedly reported to his maternal aunt/foster mother that his father had struck him so hard, he (the child) was knocked to the floor. The child also made the same statement to an investigator from the ACS Office of Confidential Investigations (OCI). But the child showed no marks, and no eyewitnesses can corroborate the child's story.

I never met the child, birth mother, or putative birth father. No valid reason exists why I should be in court, since I know only the child's paperwork, and can contribute no first-hand testimony. But ACS procedures have mandated my appearance, as they mandate substantial other unproductive activities.

Meanwhile, on another bench, a female teenager sucks her thumb while caressing her nose, like an infant. Around us swirl confusion, frustration, recrimination, shrieking children, and families coping with monumental issues. Fluorescent light throws ghastly rays on dirty blue-and-yellow walls. Ceiling tiles have been stained by water leakage. The government wall clock never deviates from one minute to two.

The History of Children's Services

This is the real-deal world of children's services today, a descendant of the child-welfare state inaugurated during the Great Depression in Franklin Delano Roosevelt's first administration. To fight poverty, President Roosevelt and his brain trust devised numerous government programs. One was named Aid to Dependent Children (ADC), which mailed checks to citizens then known as "unwed mothers." ADC continues to provide money and services to children of what now are termed "single parents." The percentage of children born to single parents has increased approximately fivefold since ADC began in 1935.

What's the connection between Aid to Dependent Children and abuse or neglect? I have read records of approximately 250 children adjudicated [determined to have been] abused/neglected, and I estimate that 95 percent were raised on Aid to Dependent Children or other public assistance programs. ACS currently has 34,000 children in foster care. The national foster-care population is roughly 546,000 children.

According to records I have read, the abuse and neglect children have suffered includes beatings that resulted in broken bones and lacerations, plus burns, torture, insufficient nourishment, medical neglect in which mothers do not take sick children to free clinics, and educational neglect in which mothers do not send children to school. Some children are born with birth defects due to lack of prenatal care, despite availability of free clinics and hospitals. Other children are born HIV-positive or addicted to cocaine. Many children are voluntarily placed in government foster care by parents who can't cope with their own flesh and blood.

Most of the children on my caseload are angry, perhaps because they feel cheated out of a decent life. They suffer pain and low self-esteem, often because they know that their absentee fathers don't give a damn about them, and their mothers are too busy with outside activities, such as smoking crack. Conventional psychological and social worker theories have failed most of these children. Nothing makes an impression except Ritalin.

Of course, not all foster children are disturbed. Some not only survive foster care but even graduate from college, a testimony to their sterling inner qualities and the skills of some foster mothers. These rare success stories are paraded periodically before TV cameras, but of my approximately 50 teenagers of college age to date, only three have gone to college and none have graduated. By my count, 80 percent of my teenaged foster children are doing poorly in school—and acting out big time.

Mountains of Paperwork

Sometimes, after hours of reading case records, I want to scream or cry. I wake up in the middle of the night, thinking about these children. I sincerely want to help them. Instead, I fill out government forms.

According to my job description, I "monitor" two nongovernment welfare agencies, Episcopal Social Services and Graham-Windham, both contracted by the city to provide homes and services to the 126 foster children on my caseload. Translated from officialese, "monitoring" means reading reports written by the contract-agency social workers and signing my name at the bottom, then filling out innumerable government forms based on information in the reports. I have no idea if these reports are accurate, and apparently it doesn't matter. I must sign anyway.

Instead of regularly visiting children for whom I am legally responsible and seeing the truth with my own eyes, I do paperwork. The reason is simple: If the paperwork isn't completed, the city loses federal funds. The more government forms completed, the more federal money the city receives.

Most of the paperwork is ludicrously redundant. For example, consider Form RES 1A, which I must fill out every six months for each child. This form can require a half hour or more to prepare, because necessary data may be lacking. After digging up obscure details and filling in blanks, I submit Form RES 1A to my supervisor, who signs off, and Form RES 1A goes into the family's case record, where it serves no purpose that I can determine.

The bureaucratic rationale for Form RES 1A is that it certifies that the child still is in foster care, but why should someone think that the child has left foster care, since the child never has been discharged? I have racked my brain and consulted with three supervisors, but we can discover no reason for Form RES 1A. . . .

Whenever a problem is identified or imagined by ACS management, a new government form is designed. At least five new forms have been introduced since I began employment, and there's no end in sight. We have government forms that track other government forms! The same information is written or typed again and again, and signed by numerous layers of bureaucracy, wasting time and resources.

No matter how hard I try, I simply cannot get on top of my paperwork, and in addition I must languish at court, or travel to the far reaches of the city, such as the last stop of the A train on Lefferts Boulevard in Queens, for conferences with children who generally don't arrive. I am mandated to participate in a planning review for each of my children every six months. This is a superficial encounter by any reasonable standard, especially since the parents or children seldom show up for the appointments. . . .

Most of my fellow caseworkers and supervisors are hardworking human beings who care about children and want to improve their lives. The main barrier is an aloof management apparatus strong on public relations and paperwork, but little else. Morale among the rank and file is rock-bottom, and caseworker turnover is constant, resulting in discontinuity of child care. . . .

Designed to Fail

I have heard caseworkers say, "ACS is designed to fail." My theory is that ACS never was designed at all, but sort of grew into the current dysfunctional monstrosity.

Child welfare in New York City began officially in 1832 when laws regulating the treatment of children were passed by city government. In 1895, the city elected to deliver services through private charitable institutions, known as contract agencies. As a result, New York City foster care today consists of two entirely separate, miscommunicating, and constantly warring entities. One is the city-controlled ACS itself, a leaky, rudderless barge floating on a swamp of paperwork. The other comprises approximately 60 private foster agencies funded by tax dollars, and allegedly monitored by ACS, but in practice they operate as loose cannons on the deck of the aforementioned sinking barge.

Although there is a tendency to trace the root of every social evil to insufficient government funding, money is not the main problem with ACS. The total ACS budget is $2.1 billion annually. With around 34,000 children in foster care, it computes to a staggering $61,764 per child!

Why does New York City foster care cost more than a year at Harvard, Yale, or Princeton? Let's follow the money trail. First, an ACS field-office caseworker on government payroll is assigned to investigate a report to the state of child abuse/ neglect. If the case is "indicated," the child might enter foster care, and might be placed in a contract-agency foster boarding home or group home funded by tax dollars, but with minimal government oversight. The child then is assigned one agency social worker, who is mandated to see him/her once every two months, according to minimum standards. The agency social worker is backed up by a supervisor, the agency's assistant director and director, plus support staff and psychologists.

In addition, each foster child soon lands on the caseload of an ACS caseworker such as me, plus supervisor I, supervisor II, supervisor III, deputy manager, manager, deputy director, director, deputy commissioner, commissioner, DLS lawyers and judges, support staff, plus numerous executive-type people, including certain individuals possessing advanced social-work degrees who attend international conferences, or develop new government forms, or modify government forms already in use, or monitor caseworkers who monitor private agencies who monitor children. ACS employs roughly 8000 individuals, all requiring office space in one of the most overpriced real estate markets on the planet Earth.

Despite this multitude of government and contract-agency employees, and the annual expenditure of $61,764 per child, each child is seen only once a month by one agency social worker, and once every six months (maybe) by one ACS caseworker, in addition to receiving basic food, shelter, clothing, medical care, and an allowance (for kids over 14), according to minimum standards. You don't need an MBA to know that a huge chunk of tax dollars is devoted to bureaucracy, not children.

I have spoken with at least 40 contract-agency social workers, and they all said that they needed more visits with each child, but couldn't manage it due to overwhelming caseloads and high volumes of paperwork. One social worker explained that she could handle 15 children effectively, making certain they receive whatever they need to thrive, in addition to interviewing parents, appearing in court, and the usual filling out of paperwork. Instead she's got 32 children, all of whom need help, but must wait for services, during which time they may disrupt classrooms, punch people, join gangs, become runaways, sell drugs, get arrested, become pregnant, or go berserk.

This is no exaggeration. Foster children are a wild bunch, and by the time help arrives, it's usually too little too late.

No Easy Answers

What's the answer? First, jettison the private agencies but incorporate their foster homes into ACS and hire their social workers and supervisors. Then provide one ACS caseworker, one supervisor, and one manager for one child, with one weekly visit from the caseworker, one monthly visit from the supervisor, and one two-monthly visit from the manager, supported by a trimmed-down childcentric ACS management staff. Dump ludicrous paperwork, and assign ACS's nonproductive staffers to actual child care. These reforms would approximately double the number of frontline caseworkers available to help troubled foster children.

The cost of these reforms would not exceed the present budget, since all the above already are on the government payroll. If more frontline caseworkers were available, they could spend more time assessing needs of the children and developing remedies that could be implemented more quickly. If foster children received more rapid interventions, they might lead happier lives.

A chilling statistic I've heard often cited at ACS: More than 70 percent of NYC's homeless are graduates of city foster care. This is one colossal failure that cries for reform, but ACS's management can be as misguided as it pleases, because the public at large is not well informed about its operations. Only an ACS insider would know that my previous director, Robert Pearlman, retired about two years ago and accepted the position of director of social services at the Catholic Guardian Society, a private contract agency. What's wrong with that? Perhaps private contract agencies exist to provide employment for retired ACS management executives. Or maybe private agencies help dilute responsibility in lawsuits against the city. Or possibly ACS management prefers to deal with nonunion private agencies rather than the militant and often unreasonable Social Services Employees Union. I can think of no other excuses for this two-headed, arthritic abomination.

Preventing Child Sexual Abuse

Carol A. Plummer

In the following article, Carol A. Plummer, an expert on child abuse prevention programs, suggests that programs that provide therapy to and monitoring of sex offenders; inform educators, child-care providers, and health-care workers about the risk factors and symptoms of abuse; and educate children about safety, help-seeking, and boundaries work to prevent child sexual abuse. Although the field of sexual abuse prevention is fairly new and although it is difficult to measure the prevention of something like sexual abuse, which is often unreported, Plummer is optimistic that the prevention programs are strengthening communities and increasing public awareness of the problem. She argues that current programs are a good start, but must be supported with more federal money and more research.

Carol A. Plummer is an assistant professor of social work at Louisiana State University. Her research interests include women and coping, child abuse, trauma, mother-child relationships, and sexual assault.

Child sexual abuse is an ancient phenomenon, but neither the public nor the professional community had significant awareness of it until the 1970s. Prior to then, child sexual abuse was vastly under-reported and misunderstood by the public and minimized in the professional literature. The recognition of child sexual abuse led to both the public and professionals attempting to identify abuse in the present generation of children as well as seeking ways to end and prevent it in future generations.

In the 1970s, prevention programs already flourished for problems such as drug abuse, suicide, and unwanted pregnancy. Yet because we knew so little about child sexual abuse, preventing it demanded that we learn a great deal. First, in order to prevent abuse, it was imperative to determine what caused it, or at least what factors contributed to it. Second, the pattern of abuse dynamics (how children are selected, coerced, sworn to secrecy, and plagued with silencing guilt) needed to be carefully studied to determine how best to intervene. . . .

Child Abuse Prevention

Prevention is a tricky business. By definition, *primary prevention* occurs prior to the problem in order to prevent it. Consequently, proving that intervention prevented a specific event (an event that did not occur) is impossible, because the event may not have occurred anyway. Likewise, it is nearly impossible to prove that preventive intervention did *not* prevent the unwanted outcome. Proving prevention's effectiveness is a difficult task; proving its ineffectiveness is equally problematic.

When examining the effectiveness of prevention programs, a major concern is a definition of terms. What constitutes "abuse," "prevention," or a "program" are all open to debate. The prevailing theories regarding prevention approaches reflect the unique components operating when sexual abuse occurs. As [David] Finkelhor shows in his "four preconditions" model, for abuse to occur there must be (1) a proclivity to abuse in the offender, inadequate (2) internal and (3) external controls of that behavior, and (4) access to children. Given that all preconditions must be present for abuse to occur, intervention in any of the four arenas theoretically could prevent abuse. Yet unlike cases of physical abuse or neglect, which are likely to be discovered by a concerned adult, sexual abuse is often shielded by secrecy and/or threats, with usually only the offender and victim aware of the behavior. This means that it is important to lower children's risk of sexual abuse by educating them. While educating children to identify and respond to sexual abuse is a component of prevention programs, prevention *never* was conceptualized by program developers as solely aimed at making children responsible for keeping themselves safe. As I have noted in earlier work,

> If we inform children about sexual abuse and ways to prevent it we adults believe children can be empowered to *help* avoid or interrupt their own victimization *sometimes*. This limitation must be acknowledged. We cannot always prevent sexual abuse or exploitation of children by giving them information or skills.

A comprehensive child sexual abuse prevention program has multiple essential components: community awareness, parent education, teacher training, age-appropriate and culturally sensitive programming for children, ongoing evaluation, and necessary updates. Optimally, all parts will be strong. They will be aimed at strengthening behavioral controls of offenders, restricting access to victims, and altering the societal factors that create offenders. Regardless of program ideology or location, these components were evident from the inception of all major child sexual abuse prevention programs. And, in recent years, prevention components have expanded. New approaches include promoting healthy images of sexuality (considering not only what we are working against, but what we are aiming for), peer education, bystander responses, and messages about dealing with bullies. Others challenged us to include juvenile and adult sex offender prevention. All of these have greatly expanded the meanings and intents of child sexual abuse prevention.

While teaching children should be the last line of defense, and while comprehensive programs have multiple components, the news media—and critics of prevention—always have been most intrigued by the idea of children being told about "sex" or "saying No" to adults. Despite what programs accomplished in their totality, the image of prevention was reduced to an image of children being taught to "Say No and tell someone." This focus has neither done justice to prevention programs nor has it informed people of the breadth and depth of prevention's scope. . . .

Prevention: the Success Story

While advocating for better research on prevention with children, we must also base our definitions of effectiveness on other criteria. Sexual abuse prevention has been effective already, even without a universal scientific stamp of approval from rigorous research. Success can be claimed because we have accomplished several objectives on the way to the ultimate goal of reducing or ending sexual abuse. Although reaching our goal will take decades of commitment and action, these accomplishments justify our continued striving:

- Prevention efforts have educated millions about sexual abuse and ways it can be prevented.

- Prevention programs have educated millions of children about sexual abuse prevention, breaking the silence and eroding the ignorance that makes children vulnerable.

- Parents have become better protectors of their children as a result of their education regarding sexual abuse prevention.

- Negative consequences of prevention education for children are nil to minimal, and there is reason to believe that unanticipated outcomes have been more positive than negative.

- Some studies have shown the ability of children to utilize prevention skills in order to avoid potentially dangerous situations.

- Prevention programs often have resulted in increased reporting of abuse, perhaps stopping abuse more readily than if no information had been given to children.

- Teachers and other professionals who come into contact with children frequently have been trained to create more protective environments and to respond more helpfully if abuse is suspected.

- Prevention programs have addressed the special needs of children of a variety of ages, ability levels, and cultural groups to prevent abuse more adequately.

- The most recent studies are showing less abuse among those females who participated in a prevention program compared with those who did not participate.

Preliminary results are promising. Programs aimed at preventing child sexual abuse have made significant strides in a little over 20 years. These efforts have not been perfect and have been much easier to criticize than to create, but prevention has proven itself in each category of its endeavors. Despite political opposition, financial onslaughts, and even programmatic imperfections, prevention is desired by the public and supported by research; it deserves a chance to get the work done to make the world safer for children.

Improving Prevention

By increasing and improving research methods, it is possible to learn much more about prevention's overall impact. Several constraints have kept this from occurring rapidly and thoroughly. Whether there will be research money and who will receive the money are primary concerns. Both research academicians and prevention practitioners should participate in framing the relevant questions and interpreting results. Currently there are few dollars allocated for such research and, at the same time, a cry for more "proof."

Given the sensitive topic, the issue of access to children, the age of the subjects, and ethical considerations, studies are inherently difficult, even with adequate funding. While we need valid and reliable testing instruments, control groups, and longitudinal data collection in order to examine program effectiveness, the major question facing prevention programs is one of survival: Given funding cuts, will we have programs to evaluate—programs with the quality and longevity needed to make possible a fair evaluation of prevention?

Methodological issues continue to pose challenges for researchers of prevention programs. However, pointing to research and shouting, "Inadequate!" should not be a substitute for preventive efforts to protect children from a real and present danger.

Prevention professionals must listen carefully to legitimate concerns about the problems with current prevention efforts. . . . Certainly, prevention advocates agree that there is a need to conduct more research, improve weak programs, place more responsibility on adults, examine possible negative effects, and deal with the fact that knowledge gain does not necessarily translate to skill usages. . . . Prevention proponents must ask of our critics: Are your criticisms really about the specifics of our programs, or are they about the concept of prevention itself? And, what are *you* doing to try to prevent abuse? Answers to these questions can help us to sort out valid from invalid criticisms.

Racial and Economic Disparities in the Child Welfare System

Nina Williams-Mbengue and Steve Christian

The following article discusses the overrepresentation of children of color in the child welfare system. Not only are children of color overrepresented, the authors contend, but African American, Latino, and Native American children are generally treated differently than are white children who enter the child welfare system. Recognizing that no one approach will solve the complicated racial and economic issues that result in different treatment, the authors, who work on child welfare and kinship care issues for the National Council of State Legislatures (NCSL), note that states such as Michigan are using strategies to prevent foster placement, provide more support for relative caregivers such as grandparents, and include the family in decision making about what services are most helpful and appropriate to their situation. The authors contend that on all levels, staff needs to be more diverse and trained in cultural competence.

The NCSL is a bipartisan organization that serves the legislators and staffs of the nation's fifty states, commonwealths, and territories. NCSL provides research, technical assistance, and opportunities for policy makers to exchange ideas on the most pressing state issues and advocates for the interests of state governments before Congress and federal agencies.

Thirty-three percent of kids in foster care are African American, but they make up only 15 percent of the child population. Yet federal studies indicate that child abuse and neglect is actually lower for black families than it is for whites.

Why the disparity?

Lawmakers in a number of states are requiring answers, and social service agencies are doing some difficult soul searching. One of the major questions is whether the nation's child welfare system undermines the strength of families, particularly families of color.

The statistics are troubling. A series of large, federally mandated studies found that parents of color are no more likely than white parents to abuse or neglect their children and showed no significant difference in overall maltreatment rates between black and white families. In fact, an analysis of the 1993 National Incidence Study of Child Abuse and Neglect by Westat researchers found that rates of maltreatment for black families are lower than rates for white families, once we control for other factors, says Robert H. Hill, a senior researcher at Westat, a research corporation based in Maryland.

Economic and Racial Disparities

Some people believe the issue is economic, not racial. African American families and neighborhoods are disproportionately poor, and poverty is highly correlated with a higher risk of child abuse.

Overrepresentation in the child welfare system may have more to do with poverty and its related social problems such as substance abuse and single parenthood than it does with race. "The available studies do not allow us to identify causes," says Hill. "You can't assume that racial differences are the result of bias or racism. On the other hand, some racial differences may indeed result from race-related factors. At this point, we just don't know."

Although racial bias may not be the cause of overrepresentation in child welfare, it is clear that black families and children are treated differently than whites once they are in the system. Studies have shown that families of color receive fewer and lower quality services, fewer contacts by caseworkers, and less access to mental health and drug treatment services. Black and Hispanic children are twice as likely as white children to be placed with relatives, and yet relative foster parents tend to get less training and fewer support services than do non-relative foster parents.

"There is widespread agreement that, compared to white children and families in the child welfare system, children of color and their families have less access to services and their outcomes are poorer," says Peter Pecora, senior director of research for Casey Family Programs, a private operating foundation based in Seattle.

Several studies have also shown that children of color are more likely to be removed from home and to remain in foster care longer, and are less likely to be returned to their parents than are white children.

Making Racial Equity a Priority

Raising these issues, let alone solving them, can be a challenge. But it is an important first step toward change.

"Action begins when state or local leaders identify racial inequities as a serious problem and resolve to address it," says Ernestine Jones, a child welfare researcher at Howard University. Jones is involved in a national initiative called the Casey-CSSP Alliance for Racial Equity in Child Welfare. Jones recently completed a study of 10 jurisdictions working on the problem. They include sites in San Francisco; San Antonio, Texas; Sioux City, Iowa; King County, Wash.; and Guilford and Wake counties in North Carolina. Programs in Connecticut, Illinois, Michigan and Minnesota were also part of the study.

"What we learned is that impetus for action can come from inside or outside the child welfare agency, but that it seems most powerful when it comes from both," she says.

While the work of each jurisdiction studied by Jones is different, she did find similarities.

All 10, for example, are reviewing data to see how decisions made at key points in the process—such as whether to investigate, to confirm or "substantiate" abuse, or to remove a child from home—may contribute to racial overrepresentation. All the sites have invited participation by parents, neighborhood residents and key agencies and other community partners. And all are working to improve decision-making, services and supports for families.

Making Child Safety a Priority

King County, Wash., for example, is using teams made up of extended family, friends, foster parents and others who are important to the family, to decide if a child should be removed from home, moved from one foster home to another, be reunited with parents, or adopted. One of the goals of this strategy, which is being used in a growing number of states, is to ensure that key decisions are based on a child's safety needs, not on race.

San Francisco is working harder to connect families reported for less serious maltreatment, such as educational neglect, with community-based services to avoid removing children from their homes. This approach allows caseworkers to help a family solve their problems instead of being subjected to an adversarial investigation when a child's safety is not at risk. Again, one of the purposes of this approach is to help families come up with their own solutions to problems such as homelessness or substance abuse, with the help of family and community resources.

Recognizing that many children of color in child welfare are cared for by relatives, Illinois pioneered the use of subsidized guardianship. Many relative foster parents don't want to adopt the children in their care, but are comfortable with legal guardianship, which does not extinguish all of a parent's legal rights. Providing monthly payments to relative guardians allows the state to convert temporary foster placements to permanent homes, maintaining family ties and reducing the number of minority children in out-of-home care.

Legislative Responses

Jones also found that most of the states she studied had "institutionalized" the work on racial disparities by enacting legislation or changing agency policy. "Legislatures in Michigan, Minnesota and Texas, for example, have really put this issue on the front burner," she says.

Michigan Senator Bill Hardiman says his state created and funded a task force to examine why more children of color are in the system. "The statistics don't lie," Hardiman says. "We need to help strengthen families. We need to discuss the issue and investigate further. We need training for child protective services and other workers."

The FY [fiscal year] 2005 budget for the Michigan Department of Human Services [DHS] included a new requirement to "address the ongoing and nationally pervasive problem of the over-representation of children of color." The department convened an advisory committee of legislators, parents, Human Services staff, tribal leaders, judges, service providers, the NAACP [National Association for the Advancement of Colored People], child advocates and others. Marianne Udow, DHS director, says support from the Legislature was key. "It was hard for people to talk about, but the leadership of Senator Hardiman and the Legislature led to a broad-based task force that held focus groups and public hearings around the state to understand this issue."

After a year of pouring over state data, hearing from national experts, reviewing national statistics and interviewing families and others throughout the state, the committee determined that African American children were more likely than white children to be removed from their homes, experience numerous foster placements, stay in care for long periods, and end up in the juvenile justice system.

In response, the Michigan Department of Human Services is now improving support for relative caregivers, using early intervention to prevent foster placement, training staff on cultural differences, and strengthening efforts to give families a say in the services they receive.

Native American Children

Although most studies have focused on African American children, Native American children are also overrepresented in child welfare. A long history of federal and state policies of assimilation, forced removal and termination of parental rights have had a devastating impact on tribes. National studies conducted between 1969 and 1974 found that 25 percent to 35 percent of Indian children in some states were living in non-Indian foster homes, adoptive homes or institutions.

In response, Congress passed the Indian Child Welfare Act of 1978 to protect the interests of Indian children. It attempted to promote the stability and security of Indian tribes and families by granting jurisdiction over children on Indian reservations to tribal courts to ensure that Indian children maintain connections with family, tribe and culture.

Enforcement by courts and child welfare agencies, however, has been inconsistent. In addition, tribes can receive federal foster care funds only through state-tribal agreements, which only a few tribes have entered into. In recent years, Arizona, California, Colorado, Iowa, Maine, Montana, New Mexico and South Dakota have passed laws to protect a child's tribal connections, strengthen compliance with the federal act, test tribal delivery of child welfare services, and prioritize placement options for Indian children removed from home.

Need for Cultural Sensitivity

The Washington Legislature has also recently focused on tribal child welfare. Representative John McCoy, a Native American, and Representative Eric Pettigrew are working to give tribes more autonomy over their child welfare systems.

"Last session we enacted a tribal foster care bill," McCoy says. "We are also working on building more compacts between the tribes and the Department of Social and Health Services." The 2006 legislation allows Indian tribes to enter into agreements with the state to license child placement agencies located on or near reservations. It also permits tribes to define the terms under which they may license agencies.

Representative McCoy says changes in the training of caseworkers and day-to-day practices are also needed. "Culturally sensitive professional staff are important," he says.

McCoy also believes that Indian children and families will benefit if tribes are given more autonomy and control over the fate of their children. "If we let the tribes do it, they'll keep kids safe from abuse," he says.

Washington's Department of Social and Health Services is developing a new child welfare model using tribal input, says director Robin Arnold Williams. Tribal members are involved in a state-level advisory committee and have been hired as state and regional staff. The department and tribal leaders have also established information and consultation protocols for sharing information and developing policy.

Steps for a Colorblind System

There is no single approach that will solve the problems of disparate treatment in child welfare. States and communities, however, are discovering that by recognizing and addressing this issue all children and families involved in the system benefit. Legislators now have more resources—a growing list of state examples, more sources of technical assistance, better data, and heightened public awareness of the need for action.

Studies in Michigan, Minnesota and Texas recommend these action steps for improving child welfare programs.

- Hire more diverse staff.

- Engage families through the use of family group conferencing.

- Train staff in cultural differences.

- Evaluate the cultural awareness of service providers.

- Track services offered to children and families by race.

- Strengthen kinship care programs and services.

- Develop state and local teams to monitor potential problems.

- Increase recruitment of foster and adoptive families of color.

- Contract with service providers of color.

Protecting Children from Exploitation on the Internet

Michael McGrath

In the following article, Michael McGrath argues that because the Internet is prevalent in most children's lives and because children's Internet use is largely unsupervised, they are vulnerable to sexual solicitation and other forms of harassment from adult Internet users. After noting various ways in which children have been victimized via the Internet, McGrath offers recommendation on how parents can best protect children from online sexual solicitation, exploitation by online child pornography, and in rare instances, abduction by someone who has befriended them via the Internet.

Michael McGrath is a clinical associate professor of psychiatry at the University of Rochester Medical Center and associate chair for ambulatory services in the Department of Psychiatry and Behavioral Health at Unity Health Systems in Rochester, New York. McGrath specializes in forensic psychiatry and criminal profiling. He is a founding member of the Academy of Behavioral Profiling.

In the United States, nearly every child has access to the Internet at home, at school, at friends' homes, at the local library, at an Internet café, or at all of those places. Security and supervision of children's Internet use vary widely. For instance, Internet access at an elementary or middle school is usually filtered and closely supervised. On the other hand, many public libraries use no filtering and do not supervise Internet use. Many parents are completely naive regarding the potential dangers to their children posed by the Internet. Par-

Michael McGrath, MD, "Cyber Victims," *Investigating Child Exploitation and Pornography: The Internet, the Law, and Forensic Science.* Burlington, MA: Elsevier Academic Press, 2005, pp. 41–47. Copyright © 2005 Elsevier B.V. All rights reserved. Reproduced with permission from Elsevier.

ents often have a completely different Internet experience than their children. Parents use the Internet mostly for e-mail, shopping, and research. Children use the Internet to communicate with people using Instant Messaging, chat, and e-mail; participate in interactive games; download music; do their homework; and perform all sorts of other activities. Today children live a large share of their lives in the virtual world. Unfortunately, the increased exposure to inappropriate content and contact with people often leads to children being victimized.

Victimization Is Unfortunately Common

According to a survey conducted through New Hampshire University, between August 1999 and February 2000, of 1,501 youths aged 10 to 17 who regularly use the Internet in the year prior to the survey:

- About one in five received some form of sexual solicitation over the Internet.

- One in thirty-three received an aggressive sexual solicitation (request to meet, talk by phone, etc.).

- One in four was exposed to unwanted pictures of nudity or sexual activity.

- One in seventeen felt threatened or harassed (not related to sexual content).

- Girls were targeted at about twice the rate boys were targeted.

- Seventy-seven percent of targeted youth were over fourteen years old.

- Although 22 percent of targeted youth were ages ten to thirteen, this group was disproportionately distressed by the incident.

- Adults (most between the ages of eighteen and twenty five) accounted for 24 percent of the sexual solicitations.

- Juveniles made 48 percent of the solicitations and 48 percent of the aggressive solicitations.

- Age was unknown for 27 percent of solicitors.

- Slightly more than two thirds of solicitations and on-line approaches came from males.

- One quarter of aggressive approaches were by females.

While not all the youth who received some sort of sexual solicitation online were bothered by the interaction, some (one in four of those solicited) were "very or extremely upset or afraid." The researchers found that few distressing online interactions are reported to parents, let alone police. To make matters more frustrating, even if parents report online harassment of their children, most police departments are ill equipped to follow up on such complaints and may view complaining parents as a nuisance. Issues of jurisdiction and arrest aside, most police departments lack the sophisticated computer skills required to retrieve digital evidence that will pass muster in court. Additionally, parents may balk at turning over their computer to police, either due to the inconvenience involved (including loss of the computer for a period of time) or possibly due to a fear that police may find something illegal on the hard drive and charge a member of the household with a crime. It is common knowledge that online child pornography arrests have stemmed from a computer being brought into a shop for repairs.

Victims and Predators

Using the same data collected in the New Hampshire study, researchers explored common characteristics of children they considered at risk for online sexual solicitation. Researchers found that girls, older teens, troubled youth, frequent Internet users, chat room participants, and children who communicate online with strangers were more likely than other children to be solicited online for sex.

A Florida man who owned and operated residential facilities for youths aged eleven to eighteen was arrested after he brought his computer in for repairs and child pornography was found on the hard drive. A well-known rock performer, Gary Glitter, was convicted in Britain of possessing child pornography after a repair shop discovered it on his hard drive. South Dakota (along with several other states) has passed a law requiring computer-repair shops to report any child pornography to authorities.

Even without a law in place, many law-abiding individuals are fearful about having contact with anything resembling child pornography and will report such findings quickly to law enforcement. Unfortunately, such community vigilantism can be overdone. There may be developing a societal zero tolerance for pictures of children that in a different era would never have even raised an eyebrow. While there is an expectation that illegal photos of children will be reported to police, there is no guidance to the photo lab as to where to draw the line, if at all. Various fairly innocuous photos have at times resulted in police action.

The online victim of the child molester is not really any different from the real-world victim, other than the fact that the victim is old enough to know how to use a computer and sufficiently literate to interact online. Such children generally tend to have low self-esteem, lack of (online) supervision, dysfunctional families, etc. While all of these traits may be common to the online victim, they are not required. An A-student with excellent self-esteem and a wonderful home life is not exempt from victimization by an online sexual predator. For example, a thirteen-year-old Minnesota eighth grader met a man she believed was eighteen through an AOL chat room before Christmas. They talked by phone prior to New Year's Eve, and she agreed to meet him near her home. She met a forty-year-old man who took her to a motel and gave her video games to play and wine coolers to drink. The man then allegedly raped the girl when she resisted his advances. A fifteen-year-old girl was found with a forty-three-year-old psychology professor in a New York State park, allegedly engaged in sexual intercourse in a car. The professor and the victim met online.

Victims Can Be Uncooperative

As noted earlier, the victim of an online sexual predator may have cooperated with the offender in one manner or another and may not cooperate with law enforcement. The victim may feel a sense of loyalty to the offender, may have participated in crimes (i.e., downloaded or traded child pornography), or may be simply generally rebellious and not fazed by the fact that [she]/he has been exploited. It may be difficult for investigators and prosecutors to relate to such a victim. Often, such a victim makes for a less than optimal witness. It is important for law enforcement personnel to refrain from being judgmental and accept the fact that gaining the cooperation of the victim may take a considerable amount of time. Judgmental treatment, disdain, and lack of interest by law enforcement toward such victims only reinforce their poor self-image and further victimize them for acts they engaged in but were poorly prepared for emotionally and were unable to give true informed consent. In an investigation of ten children identified through seized child pornography, for example, none of the ten reported the abuse they had endured to anyone without prompting.

The victims of the online sexual predator described above may differ somewhat from the victims of child pornography, whose pictures are distributed over the Internet. The victims described above are likely still living in the home, although that is no guarantee of safety. Child pornography victims are of various types: children and adolescents exploited by their guardians; victims offered alcohol and/or drugs and either videotaped without their knowledge committing sexual acts or performing under various kinds of ruses or threats; runaways seeking shelter or friendship with adolescents. The moral bankruptcy of those willing to exploit others knows no bounds. There are even clubs composed of parents who swap child pornography involving their own children with other like-minded individuals and child pornography distributors. It has been reported that live child-sex shows have even been sent over the Internet with viewers forwarding instructions to the adult participants as to what they would like to happen. . . .

How to Protect Children Online

It is not possible to ensure our children are safe from everyone at all times. But it is possible to take reasonable steps to protect our children while online. When we rely solely on educating children about Internet safety, we inadvertently place the responsibility for protecting our children on our children. Protecting children is the responsibility of their parents, the community, and government. Prevention efforts should incorporate components that educate parents, children, police officers, teachers, and health-care professionals.

Organizations such as the National Center for Missing and Exploited Children, PedoWatch, the Child Protection and Advocacy Coalition, getnetwise, and isafe offer information on how to protect children online and where to report trafficking in child pornography. Commercial software can monitor online behaviors, including e-mail, chat room conversations, instant messages, passwords, and Web site visits. Some software can even record keystrokes. Most monitoring software allows the installer to guard access to it with a password, and monitoring takes place unbeknownst to the user. The installer usually has the option of directing the monitoring software to send a report via e-mail that details all computer activity. Some monitoring software allows the installer to monitor the computer user's activity in real time from a remote location. Other software is engineered to allow the installer to conduct a forensic examination of the user's computer system from a remote location.

Common-Sense Steps

A frequently invoked misnomer in the online safety field is the concept of a "stranger." It is quite difficult to educate young children about the dangers of strangers when talking about the Internet. A stranger is someone a child does not know. Stranger-hood is easily overcome by child molesters. Even something as simple as using the child's name (perhaps overheard moments before) or asking for help in finding a lost puppy has been enough to overcome intensive "stranger danger" instruction by parents. Adolescents, on the other hand, have already had much experience dealing with adults they do not know. Prevention education efforts are well advised to encourage children and adolescents to feel comfortable in going to their parents or a trusted adult when in need of guidance. Teaching a child to "check with mom, dad, or a trusted adult" before going off with anyone is more helpful than saying, "don't ever talk to strangers." After all, if abducted, a child may be best served by turning to a stranger for help.

It is good to keep in mind that child abduction in general and Internet child molester abductions are actually rare phenomena. A child molester may be just as likely to meet an FBI agent at the planned rendezvous as a thirteen-year-old girl. While the problem of online predation is real, parents should not be in constant dread that their children will be attacked through the computer. They need to be aware of their children's online habits and who their friends are. It probably makes the most sense to educate children to the fact that some people in the world are willing to exploit them and, that when troubled by an interaction online (or in the real world), they should not be embarrassed to discuss the situation with a parent or other responsible adult.

Ten Years after Megan's Law, Children Are Not Much Safer

Alexis Jetter

On July 29, 1994, a seven-year-old New Jersey girl, Megan Nicole Kanka, was brutally raped and murdered by a two-time sex offender who had recently been released from prison. Later that year, New Jersey initiated the first Megan's Law, which provides specific mandates for active community notification so that the community is made aware of the presence of convicted sex offenders posing a risk to public safety. In May 1996 Congress passed a federal version of Megan's Law that requires states to release information to the public about known sex offenders when they are considered a risk to public safety. In the following article, written in 2006, Alexis Jetter, a freelance writer and co-editor of the Politics of Motherhood, *considers how well, ten years after its establishment, Megan's Law is protecting children from sex offenders and suggests that states, schools, communities, and parents need to continue to improve the effectiveness of Megan's Law.*

Shortly after her son started kindergarten, Nadine K. got a letter from the local school district. Mistaking it for a notice about a book fair, Nadine opened the envelope in front of the boy and his two-year-old sister. What she read gave her the chills: A convicted child molester, whom police considered likely to strike again, was living in her Long Island, New York, neighborhood. There was no address, no details about the perpetrator or his crimes—only a grainy, poorly photocopied mug shot of a man she didn't recognize. Oh my God, Nadine thought to herself, not breathing. This is real, and it's right around the corner.

Alexis Jetter, "The Sex Offender is STILL Next Door," *Good Housekeeping*, vol. 246, issue 1, January 2006, pp. 153–58. Reproduced by permission of the author.

"What is it, Mommy?" her son asked. "It's nothing," Nadine said hastily. Heart pounding, she put the letter atop a high china cabinet. What am I supposed to do with this? she wondered, trying not to panic. A New York City advertising executive, Nadine was used to dealing with high-stakes pressure. But this danger had come out of the blue—and had targeted her children.

Megan's Law

Nadine K. got that alert because of Megan's Law, named after a seven-year-old New Jersey girl who was raped and strangled in 1994 by a convicted sex offender who lived across the street. The legislation requires sex offenders to register their addresses with local police or state officials (and notify the authorities if they move). It also requires states to release information about convicted sex offenders to the public. And that can be a mixed blessing.

"You really feel helpless," says Nadine. "You have this information, but what are you going to do to keep your child safe?" In a subsequent alert from the school, Nadine was directed to a group called Parents for Megan's Law for more information. On the organization's Web site, she plugged in her zip code—and up jumped the faces of several more sex criminals living nearby. "The fear came right back," she says. "It reminded me that these people are out there, and they seem to have more rights than my children."

Megan's Law Helps Track and Catch Child Molesters

Almost everyone agrees that Megan's Law, which turns ten this year [2006], has made a difference. Across the country, it has helped stop sexual predators before they can score fresh victims. In Seattle, a mom acting on a hunch called the city police department's Sex and Kidnapping Offender Detail and learned that a man masquerading as a tutor for her two young daughters was a child molester with a long rap sheet. In California, a mother contacted a Megan's Law information line and discovered that her child's coach had been convicted of molesting children. Also in California, a golf course manager found out that an employee who had direct contact with children had been convicted of performing lewd or lascivious acts with a child under 14. And Megan's Law can also help police catch registered sex offenders if they strike again.

"A lot of things work about Megan's Law," insists Mary Coffee, planning and policy administrator for the Florida Department of Law Enforcements sex-offender registry. "There are known sexual offenders who are living among the public. Citizens made it clear that they want to have this information to make decisions for their families."

Yet most parents, like Nadine K., get almost no direction on what to do once they learn there's a molester in their midst. As Bob Shilling, the lead detective for [the] Seattle Police Department Sex and Kidnapping Offender Detail, puts it: "You can't do community notification without community education. It's like smoking a cigarette in a pool of gasoline."

Loopholes in Megan's Law

Beyond that, huge loopholes in Megan's Law cripple its effectiveness. A gruesome spate of child rape/murders made headlines last year—and according to Kim English, research director for the Colorado Division of Criminal Justice, at least three of the perpetrators were registered. Here are some of the law's most serious problems:

No one has to tell you anything. "The spirit of Megan's Law is that, if a sex offender moves into your neighborhood, you'll be notified," says Laura Ahearn, executive director of Parents for Megan's Law. "That is not the case." The law doesn't require police to actually notify parents when a sex offender moves nearby or to monitor his movements—only to make information about the molester available to the public. Although some states, like Washington, provide "active" notification about resident sex offenders (through mailings, posted flyers, newspaper alerts, and community meetings), most rely on "passive" notification—namely, sex-offender Web sites. That puts the onus on parents to get the information they need. And most school districts don't notify parents when a convicted sex offender moves in (Nadine K.'s district was an exception).

Not all convicted sex offenders are registered. Most state registries exclude offenders whose crime, no matter how heinous, predates the law's 1996 passage. And they don't track the very large group of sexual predators who plea-bargained down to misdemeanors not involving sexual contact. That means shorter prison sentences for these molesters—often no more than what they'd get for "stealing a pair of sneakers from Kmart," says Kenneth Rau, chief of detectives of the Suffolk County, New York, police department. More alarming, their convictions don't flag them as sex offenders—so they're not on Megan's Law registries. Another problem: Juveniles, who commit almost half of all acts of molestation on victims under 12, are usually not required to register or to be listed on state sex-offender Web sites. "I think the invisible predator population out there is a tremendous threat," says Rau.

Red tape can snarl the works. One Long Island woman found out that her tenant, who was babysitting her two young sons, was a convicted child molester only when she intercepted a letter from the New York State Division of Criminal Justice Services. She checked the state registry, but the man wasn't there. Then she contacted Parents for Megan's Law and learned that the man was a convicted sex offender—in Alabama. New York hadn't yet assessed his risk level, so he wasn't in the system. "A sex offender who moves from one state to another may not be added to the new state's register for months, even years," says Ahearn, of Parents for Megan's Law. "We know plenty of dangerous sexual offenders who aren't on the Web sites." More frightening, this year, tens of thousands will drop off the map—having completed the original ten-year registration requirement.

Risk assessment is dicey. Many states assign three levels of risk to sex offenders leaving prison, ranging from one, meaning they pose a low risk of reoffending, to three, meaning high risk. But assigning risk is inexact and sometimes misguided. In 2002, 14-year-old Kristen Jackson of Wooster, Ohio, was brutally raped, murdered, and dismembered by a convicted child rapist and kidnapper who had been labeled low risk when he was released from prison six months earlier. As a result of that label, the community was not informed that he was living one block from Kristen's home. "For the most cunning of criminals, you can't predict if they're going to reoffend," says Ahearn.

Many law-enforcement officials believe that all sex offenders should be treated as high risk, placed on lifetime registries, and supervised by either probation or police officers. But supervision is a difficult proposition when you consider that there are over half a million registered sex offenders in the United States (not to mention perhaps hundreds of thousands of unregistered ones, according to Scott Maison, a researcher at the Department of Justice's Center for Sex Offender Management).

Congress recently moved to strengthen Megan's Law through a new measure. Among other things, it would improve the tracking of sex offenders across state lines and help fund electronic-bracelet-monitoring in several states.

Parents and Schools Need to Take Initiative

But new laws won't solve all the problems, warns Carolyn Atwell Davis, legislative director of the National Center for Missing & Exploited Children. "Call your school's superintendent," she says. "Tell her: 'I want a safety education program in my school.' It needs to be done a couple of times a year, aimed at parents as well as children. That's the missing link."

Which brings us back to Nadine K. Though she firmly believes that the government and police should be doing more, she understands now that she will have to do more herself. She's been handing out information from child advocacy groups to her friends with tips on how to protect kids. And she's talked to her own children—so far, with limited success. "I told my kids that there are some bad men living nearby and they have to be careful. But they don't get it. They think every bad guy looks like the villain in the cartoons. These men look like everybody at the mall."

Nadine lets out a small, dry laugh. The file of sex-offender alerts on her china cabinet is still growing, she says, but there's one notice she'd really like to get someday. "They never tell you when one of these guys moves out," she says. "That would be a nice letter to get."

Chronology

1639

The earliest recorded trial for child abuse in the American colonies. A master in Salem, Massachusetts, is charged with killing his apprentice.

1641

Nathaniel Ward of the Massachusetts Bay Colony composes the *Body of Liberties*, which contains the first laws anywhere in the world against wife beating and "unnatural severitie" to children.

1693

British philosopher John Locke publishes his influential *Some Thoughts Concerning Education*, in which he argues that because the pain that accompanies a whipping is generally remembered more than the reason for punishment, it is more effective to use reason to bend a child's will to submission toward the parents.

1836

Massachusetts passes a law stating that children who work must receive at least three months of schooling per year.

1848

Pennsylvania makes it illegal for children under age twelve to work in factories.

1874

Etta Angell Wheeler discovers a malnourished, physically abused child in a Hell's Kitchen tenement in New York City and appeals to Henry Bergh for legal assistance in removing the child from the home and charging the parents with cruelty.

1875

Henry Bergh founds the American Society for the Prevention of Cruelty to Children.

1889

Jane Addams founds Hull House to provide services for poor children and their families.

1890

Jacob Riis publishes *How the Other Half Lives: The Children of the Poor* follows in 1892.

1896

Sigmund Freud publishes "On the Aetiology of Hysteria," in which he argues that early childhood sexual abuse is the source of adult mental illness among his clients. He recants this position the following year.

1899

The first juvenile court system in the United States was established in Chicago, Illinois, on July 1, 1899.

1904

The National Child Labor Committee [NCLC] is formed to draw public attention to the exploitation of children. The NCLC included such activists as Jane Addams and Lewis Hines.

1909

William Healy establishes the first child guidance clinic for juvenile delinquents. Located in Chicago it employed a team of psychiatrists, social workers, and psychologists.

1912

Congress establishes the Children's Bureau. The stated purpose of the new bureau is to investigate and report "upon all matters pertaining to the welfare of children and child life among all classes of our people."

1935

Congress enacts the Social Security Act, which includes limited funds for child welfare services under Title V, "Grants to States for Maternal and Child Welfare."

1938

The federal Fair Labor Standards Act is approved. It outlaws labor by children under age sixteen.

1961

C. Henry Kempe and colleagues coin the term *battered child syndrome* to describe intentional injuries to children.

1969

State participation in the Title IV-A Aid to Families with Dependent Children (AFDC) foster care program is made mandatory.

1972

The C. Henry Kempe National Center for Prevention and Treatment of Child Abuse and Neglect is founded to address child abuse prevention and treatment.

1974

Congress passes the Child Abuse Prevention and Treatment Act (CAPTA). It is the only federal legislation exclusively dedicated to the prevention, assessment, identification, and treatment of child abuse and neglect.

1989

The General Assembly of the United Nations ratifies the Convention on the Rights of the Child, which stipulates, on an international level, that governments have a responsibility to ensure that children's rights are not violated and are "respected, protected, and fulfilled." The United States is one of the few countries to not ratify the convention.

1994

Legislation is enacted that directs the U.S. Department of Health and Human Services to create a new review of state child welfare systems. This directive ultimately creates the Child and Family Service Reviews. The legislation also authorizes child welfare waiver demonstrations.

1995

Congress passes the Sex Crimes Against Children Prevention Act.

1996

Congress enacts Megan's Law, which requires that sex offenders appear in a public directory.

1996

The Temporary Assistance for Needy Families (TANF) block grant is created thus eliminating Aid to Families with Dependent Children [AFDC] as an individual entitlement. While TANF replaces AFDC, the law requires states to continue to base Title IV-E Foster Care and Adoption Assistance eligibility on AFDC standards in place on July 16, 1996.

1997

The Adoption and Safe Families Act is enacted. It creates timelines for moving children to permanency, provides adoption bonuses for states, and continues the child welfare waiver demonstrations. The law also renames the Family Preservation and Family Support program to Promoting Safe and Stable Families (PSSF) and expands the use of funds to two additional categories of service: time-limited reunification services and adoption promotion and support services.

1999

The Independent Living program is expanded and renamed in honor of Senator John H. Chafee (R-RI).

2001

Promoting Safe and Stable Families is reauthorized. The law also amends the John H. Chafee Independent Living program to provide funding for education and training vouchers for foster youth and create new funding for mentoring of children of incarcerated parents.

2002

The Catholic Church in the United States is plunged into scandal as it becomes known that officials in many dioceses across the country had been covering up sexual abuse of children by their priest for years rather than taking constructive action to end the abuse.

Organizations to Contact

The editors have compiled the following list of organizations concerned with the issues debated in this book. The descriptions are derived from materials provided by the organizations. All have publications or information available for interested readers. The list was compiled on the date of publication of the present volume; the information provided here may change. Be aware that many organizations take several weeks or longer to respond to inquiries, so allow as much time as possible.

ACT for Kids
7 South Howard, Suite 200, Spokane, WA   99201
(509) 747-8224 • fax: (509) 747-0609
e-mail: info@actforkids.org
Web site: www.actforkids.org

ACT for Kids is a nonprofit organization that provides resources, consultation, research, and training for the prevention and treatment of child abuse and sexual violence. The organization's publications include workbooks, manuals, and the books *My Very Own Book About Me* and *How to Survive the Sexual Abuse of Your Child*.

**American Academy of Child and
Adolescent Psychiatry (AACAP)**
3615 Wisconsin Avenue NW, Washington, DC   20016
(202) 966-7300 • fax: (202) 966-2891
Web site: www.aacap.org

The AACAP supports and advances child and adolescent psychiatry through research and the distribution of information. The academy's goal is to provide information that will ensure proper treatment for children who suffer from mental or behavioral disorders due to child abuse, molestation, or other issues. The AACAP publishes fact sheets on a variety of issues concerning disorders that affect children and adolescents.

American Professional Society on the Abuse of Children (APSAC)
407 South Dearborn, Suite 1300, Chicago, IL 60605
(312) 554-0166 • fax: (312) 554-0919
e-mail: APSACMems@aol.com
Web site: www.apsac.org

The APSAC is dedicated to improving the coordination of services in the fields of child abuse prevention, treatment, and research. It publishes a quarterly newsletter, the *Advisor*, and the *Journal of Interpersonal Violence*.

Childhelp USA
15757 North Seventy-eighth Street, Scottsdale, AZ 85260
hotline: (480) 922-8212 (800) 4-A-Child
Web site: www.childhelpusa.org

Childhelp USA is an organization dedicated to helping victims of child abuse and neglect. The organization operates a hotline that victims can call twenty-four-hours-a-day to speak with professional counselors. Childhelp also operates treatment facilities and regional centers that provide services to abused children.

Child Welfare Information Gateway
Children's Bureau/ACYF
1250 Maryland Avenue SW, Eighth Floor
Washington, DC 20024
(703) 385-7565
e-mail: info@childwelfare.gov
Web site: www.childwelfare.gov

The Child Welfare Information Gateway national clearinghouse collects, catalogues, and disseminates information on all aspects of child maltreatment, including identification, prevention, treatment, public awareness, training, and education. It also offers various reports, fact sheets, and bulletins concerning child abuse and neglect.

False Memory Syndrome Foundation
3401 Market Street, Suite 130, Philadelphia, PA 19104

(215) 387-1865 • fax: (215) 387-1917
Web site: www.fmsfonline.org

The False Memory Syndrome Foundation believes that many
"delayed memories" of sexual abuse are the result of false
memory syndrome (FMS). In FMS, patients in therapy "recall" childhood abuse that never occurred. The foundation
seeks to discover the real reasons for the spread of FMS, works
for the prevention of new cases, and aids FMS victims, including those falsely accused of abuse. The foundation publishes a
newsletter and various papers and distributes articles and information on FMS.

National Center for Missing & Exploited Children (NCMEC)
699 Prince Street, Alexandria, VA   22314
(703) 274-3900 • fax: (703) 274-2200
Web sites: www.missingkids.com

The NCMEC serves as a clearinghouse of information on
missing and exploited children and coordinates child protection efforts with the private sector. It offers a number of publications on these issues, including guidelines for parents
whose children are testifying in court, and help for abused
children. In 2001 NCMEC launched the NetSmartz program
to teach children about Internet safety.

National Coalition Against Domestic Violence (NCADV)
Child Advocacy Task Force, PO Box 18749
Denver, CO   80918
(303) 389-1852 • fax: (303) 831-9251
Web site: www.ncadv.org

The NCADV represents organizations and individuals that as-
sist battered women and their children. The Child Advocacy
Task Force deals with issues affecting children who witness
violence at home or are themselves abused. It publishes the
Bulletin, a quarterly newsletter.

National Criminal Justice Reference Service (NCJRS)
U.S. Department of Justice, Rockville, MD   20849

(301) 519-5500
e-mail: askncjrs@ncjrs.org
Web site: www.ncjrs.org

A research and development agency of the U.S. Department of Justice, NCJRS was established to prevent and reduce crime and to improve the criminal justice system. Among its publications are *Resource Guidelines: Improving Court Practice in Child Abuse and Neglect Cases* and *Recognizing When a Child's Injury or Illness Is Caused by Abuse*.

New York Society for the Prevention of Cruelty to Children (NYSPCC)

161 William Street, New York, NY   10038
(212) 233-5500 • fax (212) 791-5227
Web site: www.nyspcc.org

Founded in 1875, the NYSPCC is the first child protective agency in the world. Throughout its 131-year history, the NYSPCC has sought, through the development of new and innovative programs, to meet the urgent needs of New York City's most vulnerable children. It is with this same spirit of innovation, concern, and compassion that the NYSPCC continually strives to fulfill its mission of protecting children and strengthening families through mental health, legal, and educational services.

Prevent Child Abuse America (PCAA)

200 South Michigan Avenue, Chicago, IL   60604
(312) 663-3520 • fax: (312) 939-8962
e-mail: mailbox@preventchildabuse.org
Web site: www.preventchildabuse.org

PCAA's mission is to prevent all forms of child abuse. It distributes and publishes materials on a variety of topics, including child abuse and child abuse prevention. *Talking About Child Sexual Abuse* and *Basic Facts About Child Sexual Abuse* are among the various pamphlets PCAA offers.

Rape, Abuse & Incest National Network (RAINN)

635-B Pennsylvania Avenue SE, Washington, DC   20003
(202) 544-1034 • fax: (202)-544-1401
e-mail info@rainn.org
Web site www.rain.org

RAINN is the nation's largest anti-sexual assault organization. RAINN operates the National Sexual Assault Hotline and carries out programs to prevent sexual assaults, help victims, and ensure that rapists are brought to justice. Its Web site contains statistics, counseling resources, prevention tips, news, and more.

Recovered Memory Project

Taubman Center for Public Policy and
American Institutions at Brown University
Providence, RI   02912
(401) 863-2201
e-mail: ross_cheit@brown.edu
Web site: www.brown.edu/Departments/Taubman Center/ Recovmem

The purpose of the Recovered Memory Project is to collect and disseminate information relevant to the debate over whether traumatic events can be forgotten and then remembered later in life. That debate has focused on recovered memories of childhood sexual abuse. But the phenomenon extends to other traumas, including physical abuse or witnessing a murder. The Project's Web site collects cases that support the Project's viewpoint, including clinical studies and work by cognitive psychologists. It also offers resources for survivors of trauma.

Safer Society Foundation

PO Box 340, Brandon, VT   05733
(802) 247-3132 • fax: (802) 247-4233
e-mail: ray@usa-ads.net
Web site: www.safersociety.org

The Safer Society Foundation is a national research, advocacy, and referral center for the prevention of sexual abuse of children and adults. The Safer Society Press publishes research, studies, and books on treatment for sexual victims and offenders and on the prevention of sexual abuse.

For Further Research

Books

Ola W. Barnett, Cindy L. Miller-Perrin, and Robin D. Perrin, *Family Violence Across the Lifespan: An Introduction.* Thousand Oaks, CA: Sage, 1997.

Mary Cable, *The Little Darlings: A History of Child Rearing in America.* New York: Scribner, 1975.

Matt Carroll, Kevin Cullen, Thomas Farragher, Stephen Kurkijian, Michael Paulson, Sacha Pfeiffer, Michael Rezendes, and Walter V. Robinson, *Betrayal: The Crisis in the Catholic Church.* New York: Little, Brown, 2002.

Lydia Maria Child, *The Mother's Book.* Boston: Carter, Hendee and Babcock, 1831.

Cynthia Crosson-Tower, *Understanding Child Abuse and Neglect.* Boston: Allyn & Bacon, 2005.

Anthony Fletcher and Stephen Hussey, eds., *Childhood in Question: Children, Parents and the State.* Manchester, England: Manchester University Press, 1999.

Lisa Aronson Fontes, *Child Abuse and Culture: Working with Diverse Families.* New York: Guilford Press, 2005.

David France, *Our Fathers: The Secret Life of the Catholic Church in an Age of Scandal.* New York: Broadway Books, 2005.

Sigmund Freud, *Dora: An Analysis of a Case of Hysteria.* New York: Macmillan, 1963.

Irwin A. Hyman, *Reading, Writing and the Hickory Stick: The Appalling Story of Physical and Psychological Abuse in American Schools.* Lexington, MA: Lexington Books, 1990.

Carolyn Lehman, *Strong at the Heart: How It Feels to Heal from Sexual Abuse* New York: Farrar, Straus and Giroux, 2005.

Roger J.R. Levesque, *Child Maltreatment Law: Foundations in Science, Practice, and Policy*. Durham, NC: Carolina Academic Press, 2002.

Elizabeth Loftus, *The Myth of Repressed Memory: False Memories and Allegations of Sexual Abuse* New York: St. Martin's, 1994.

Alice Miller, *The Body Never Lies: The Lingering Effects of Cruel Parenting*. Trans. Andrew Jenkins. New York: Norton, 2005.

Susan B. Miller, *When Parents Have Problems: A Book for Teens and Older Children with an Abusive, Alcoholic or Mentally Ill Parent*. Springfield, IL: Charles C. Thomas, 1995.

Gregory K. Moffatt, *Wounded Innocents and Fallen Angels: Child Abuse and Child Aggression*. Westport, CT: Praeger, 2003.

Richard B. Pelzer, *A Brother's Journey: Surviving a Childhood of Abuse*. New York: Warner Books, 2005.

Maria Piers, *Infanticide: Past and Present*. New York: Norton, 1978.

Elizabeth Pleck, *Domestic Tyranny: The Making of Social Policy Against Family Violence from Colonial Times to the Present*. New York: Oxford University Press, 1987.

Dorothy Rabinowitz, *No Crueler Tyrannies: Accusation, False Witness, and Other Terrors of Our Times*. New York: Wall Street Journal Books, 2003.

Jacob Riis, *The Children of the Poor*. New York: Scribner, 1892.

Stephen Robertson, *Crimes Against Children: Sexual Violence and Legal Culture in New York City, 1880–1960.* Chapel Hill: University of North Carolina Press, 2005.

Henry S. Salt, *The Flogging Craze: A Statement of the Case Against Corporal Punishment.* London: George Allen & Unwin, 1916.

Eric A. Shelman and Stephen Lazoritz, *The Mary Ellen Wilson Child Abuse Case and the Beginning of Children's Rights in 19th Century America.* Jefferson, NC: McFarland, 2005.

Sue William Silverman, *Because I Remember Terror. Father, I Remember You.* Athens: University of Georgia Press, 1996.

Margaret G. Smith and Rowena Fong, *Children of Neglect: When No One Cares.* New York: Brunner-Routledge, 2004.

Murray A. Straus, *Beating the Devil Out of Them: Corporal Punishment in American Families and Its Effects on Children.* New Brunswick, NJ: Transaction Publishers, 2001.

U.S. Department of Health and Human Services Administration on Children, Youth and Families, *Child Maltreatment 2005.* Washington, DC: U.S. Government Printing Office, 2006.

Fred Wulczyn, Richard P. Barth, Ying-Ying T. Yuan, Brenda Jones Harden, John Landsverk, *Beyond Common Sense: Child Welfare, Child Well-Being, and the Evidence for Policy Reform.* New Brunswick, NJ: Aldine Transaction, 2005.

Periodicals

Michael J. Bader, "Who Is Hurting the Children? The Political Psychology of Pedophilia in American Society," *Tikkun*, May–June 2003.

Daniel Bergner, "The Making of a Molester," *New York Times Magazine*, January 23, 2005.

Agostino Bono, "Dealing with the Pain: Bishops and Abuse Victims Meet," *America*, November 17, 2003.

Stephen A. Califano Jr., "The Least Among Us: Children of Substance-Abusing Parents," *America*, April 24, 1999.

Patricia Chisholm, "Who Decides What's Right?" *Maclean's*, September 10, 2001.

Ta-Nehisi Paul Coates, "When Parents Are the Threat," *Time*, May 8, 2006.

Lloyd de Mause, "On Writing Childhood History," *Journal of Psychohistory*, Fall 1988.

Nikitta A. Foston, "The Shocking Story Behind the Pain Nobody Talks About: Sexual Abuse of Black Boys," *Ebony*, June 2005.

Brenda Goodman, "Forgiveness Is Good, Up to a Point: Some Abuse Victims Should Not Reconcile with Abusers," *Psychology Today*, January–February 2004.

Jerry Harris, "Drug-Endangered Children," *FBI Law Enforcement Bulletin*, February 2004.

Nat Hentoff, "Another Crucible," *Editor and Publisher*, January 1, 2001.

J.D. Heyman et al., "Did Bullying—or a Mother's Neglect—Drive a 12-Year-Old Boy To Suicide?" *People*, October 20, 2003.

Barbara J. Howard, "Take a Deep Breath When You Suspect Neglect," *Pediatric News*, April 2007.

Eric S. Janus, "Sexually Violent Predator Laws: Psychiatry in Service to a Morally Dubious Enterprise," *Lancet*, December 2004.

Gay Jervey, "The Bad Mother," *Good Housekeeping*, August 2004.

Maggie Jones, "Who Was Abused?" *New York Times Magazine*, September 19, 2004.

Kathleen Kaiser, "Look at Link Between Abuse and Unplanned Pregnancy," *South Bend Tribune*, March 14, 2004.

Leslie Kaufman and Richard Lezin Jones, "How Years of Budget Cuts Put New Jersey's Children at Risk," *New York Times*, September 23, 2003.

C. Henry Kempe, Frederic N. Silverman, Brandt F. Steele, William Droegemueller, and Henry K. Silver, "The Battered-Child Syndrome," *JAMA: The Journal of the American Medical Association*, July 1962.

Janet Kornblum, "A Tough Balance Between Kids' Safety, Offenders' Rights: Megan's Law Has Critics on Both Sides of Argument," *USA Today*, January 29, 2003.

Carolyn A. Kubitschek, "Holding Foster Care Agencies Responsible for Abuse and Neglect," *Human Rights*, Winter 2005.

Rivka Gerwitz Little, "Who's Minding the Kids?" *Village Voice*, March 25, 2003.

Bob Meadows et al., "Two Little Girls Lost, Two Tragic Endings," *People*, April 4, 2005.

Jane Mildred, "Claimsmakers in the Child Sexual Abuse 'Wars': Who Are They and What Do They Want?" *Social Work*, October 2003.

Ami Neiberger-Miller, "Exposing a Dark Secret," *Children's Voice*, March–April 2004.

Kellie Pickler, "How I Survived Child Abuse," *US Weekly*, November 27, 2006.

Thomas P. Rausch, "Where Do We Go from Here?" *America*, October 18, 2004.

Stephen J. Rossetti, "The Catholic Church and Child Sexual Abuse," *America*, April 22, 2002.

Sharon Secor, "Foster Care Crisis; Let the Numbers Speak," *Everybody's*, July–August 2004.

Clare Sheridan and Nancy Wolfe, "If Only You Hadn't, I Would Not Have Hit You: Infant Crying and Abuse," *Lancet*, October 9–15, 2004.

Suzanne Smalley and Brian Braiker, "Suffer the Children," *Newsweek*, January 20, 2003.

Margaret Talbot, "The Bad Mother; a Reporter at Large," *New Yorker*, August 9, 2004.

"Teen Tech Tormentors: What's a Parent to Do?" *eWeek*, February 16, 2007.

Martin H. Teichner, "Scars That Won't Heal: The Neurobiology of Child Abuse," *Scientific American*, March 2002.

Alex Tresniowski, "Monsters or Misjudged?" *People*, November 24, 2003.

Dawn Turner Trice, "Rescued from Neglect, 5 Brothers Find Hope," *Chicago Tribune*, February 15, 2004.

Terry Donovan Urekew, "A Victim's Defense of Priests," *Commonweal*, October 11, 2002.

Richard Wexler "Caught in a Master Narrative," *Neiman Reports*, Winter 2000.

Isabel Wolock and Bernard Horowitz, "Child Maltreatment as a Social Problem: The Neglect of Neglect," *American Journal of Orthopsychiatry*, October 1984.

Tina Wright, "Stopping the Cycle of Abuse," *Black Parenting*, June 30, 2001.

Internet Source

General Assembly of the United Nations "Convention on the Rights of the Child," November 20, 1989. http://child-abuse.com/childhouse/childwatch/cwi/ convention.html.

Index